BC

BV 601.8 .N6 1969
Noyce, Gaylord B.
The church is not expendable

The Church
Is Not Expendable

THE CHURCH IS NOT EXPENDABLE

by

Gaylord B. Noyce

The Westminster Press
Philadelphia

BV
601.8
.N8
1969

COPYRIGHT © MCMLXIX THE WESTMINSTER PRESS

All rights reserved—no part of this book may be
reproduced in any form without permission in
writing from the publisher, except by a reviewer
who wishes to quote brief passages in connection with a review in magazine or newspaper.

Scripture quotations from the Revised Standard Version
of the Bible are copyright, 1946 and 1952, by the Division of Christian Education of the National Council of
Churches, and are used by permission.

STANDARD BOOK No. 664–20849–5

LIBRARY OF CONGRESS CATALOG CARD No. 69–10900

LIBRARY
BERKELEY DIVINITY SCHOOL
NEW HAVEN 11, CONN

PUBLISHED BY THE WESTMINSTER PRESS®
PHILADELPHIA, PENNSYLVANIA
PRINTED IN THE UNITED STATES OF AMERICA

To Dotey

PREFACE

Any reality with deep significance for human life bears analysis from a number of directions, and the statement of any one perspective does not necessarily negate the truth in some other. Because of this, one can take courage as one dares yet another contribution to the current discussion on the nature and mission of the church.

This book has particular concern with the local congregation. It proposes that the unique function of the church is the articulation in word and deed of the God-relation in which men and their societies "live and move and have . . . [their] being." An understanding of how religious activity serves the needs of those within the church and the needs of the whole culture enables us to have a clearer conception of the purposes and possibilities of the Christian church. Working through such a view, the argument proceeds to look at worship and social action, at teaching and fellowship activities in the local parish with an eye to appreciation of the valid dynamics at work in present-day churches as well as to realistic proposals for church renewal.

This book is set out with a certain sense of urgency. Some contemporary assertions about the church are so grandiose as to leave us in utter despair over the churches as they are and oblivious to the worthy ends even now served by them, not to mention their potential—again, even in their present forms. Other assertions appear so single-minded, not to say shallow, in their understanding of the nature of the human spirit as to flatten it out and render unnecessary the "religious" elements that in the past have distinguished the church from other institutions serving the general good and that presumably will continue to do so in time to come. The resultant confusion begs an answer, it seems to me, in fairly simple language, to such simple questions from pulpits and pews as these: Why have churches anymore? Can the churches as we have them do any good? What is the church all about? What sense can we make of the diverse church-sponsored activities which we see around us? By looking at the local church as it presents itself, I am proposing one view—hopefully a helpful one—of that many-faceted reality which is the church.

Considerable credit for chastening a more academic style so that more people may follow this argument is due my wife and her helpful criticism. I extend my thanks also to Mrs. Judith McBride, who did the typing of the final draft. But for patience and encouragement in ministry, little is more important than the commitment of those many members in the two parishes where I began my parish service—Hancock Congregational Church in Lexington, Massachusetts, and United Church, Raleigh, North Carolina. Knowing from the inside a church that deserves the name, even while all our human frailty is very much a constant part of the picture, is what gives us a firm basis of constructive criticism and faithful hope for the church of Jesus Christ.

G. B. N.

New Haven, Connecticut

CONTENTS

Chapter One

TOWARD CREATIVE REVOLUTION

In spite of the high level of religious interest across our country, there is a persistent cadence of confusing comment about the church. Much of it leaves the impression that the local parish church is expendable.

The comment takes many forms. Often, within the Christian community, it takes up a theme from Dietrich Bonhoeffer to the effect that ours is a time when man has "come of age" and no longer needs religious forms to console him or teach him to do good. What we need today is a "religionless Christianity."

Sometimes the criticism is such a radical proposal for new forms of the church—because of the "irrelevance" of the old—that it calls for a revolution which would amount to disbanding the church as we know it today. Critics in this camp would not admit that the church was being disbanded through their revolution. They would call their arguments a lover's quarrel, an attack on the church as it is for the love of what it might become. Yet the church as we know it, as worshiping fellowship, would be so radically changed as to leave many, many Christians of the present simply lost.

Outside the Christian community, of course, many say with their actions more than with their words that the church is expendable. They stand indifferent toward the church. In a nation in which the church was oppressing men or in which there was no political gain to be harvested by friendly gestures to "the Almighty" or to the church ("Your Honor, Reverend Clergy, Honored Guests, Ladies and Gentlemen," the speaker begins), criticism of those who foster churchly activity would be more common. On the other hand, indifference insults a person more than outright hostility. When you oppose a man you show that you at least take him seriously. The actions of many institutions and of great numbers of individuals today exhibit vast indifference to the church.

To each of these three points of view—that of the anti-institutionalist, of the careless reformer, and of the indifferent in the culture at large—the answer must be given that the church is not expendable. To state our thesis in this negative proposition is not to be reactionary. Conservative it may be in the sense of seeing in some structure of the past a purpose which ought still to be served. By the same token, however, the statement can be called progressive if it steps beyond the mood of today toward a different mood we would foster for tomorrow. What we want to avoid is not a revolution, for the church needs renewal radical enough to be called just that. What we want to avoid is careless revolution that unnecessarily destroys a legacy which is still essential for the future—the congregation, the local church.

The church is not expendable. To be sure, compelling reasons for ambivalence about the religious activity of men present themselves. Important theological reasons come at the top of the list. In a book that proved to be a milestone to Western Christendom in the twentieth century, such words as these about the church burn their way across the pages: "The opposition between the Church and the Gospel is final and all-embracing; the Gospel dissolves the Church and the Church dissolves the Gospel."[1]

In these lines by Karl Barth, everything that Christians do in the religious enterprise, in "church work," is called into question. Barth is saying that nothing men on their own can do with their religion has anything to do with changing God, winning his favor, even "bringing in the Kingdom," or building any ultimately lasting righteousness on man's side as he stands before God.

Thus the task of understanding the religious enterprise is an urgent but difficult assignment. Why do we invest our energy and thought in the church?[2] Is it to save ourselves? If so, we work to our own damnation, according to the best that is in our Christian heritage—Old Testament, New Testament, and church teaching. God saves us, not man. For this reason the church is spiritually the most dangerous place for a man to be. If his life there makes him so proud that he thinks to justify himself, to be righteous before others, his life there is more a means for his downfall than for his hope. Jesus said as much in the parable of the Pharisee and the publican.

The following question then arises: "Should we abandon our congregational activity and our buildings, our study groups and our liturgies, our teas and action projects, and all our 'solemn assemblies'"? Seeing the ways in which the church "dissolves" the gospel, men may be tempted to the conclusion that we should. For good reason men do urge the abandonment of traditional churches for new forms which are just beginning to appear. One serious critic of the present middle-class churches of suburbia was heard to level this broadside at them: "I think these churches must be empty and closed before there can be much meaningful life in the church again."

We will always need new forms of the church in a changing world. They have continually cropped up in the past. After the house churches of the New Testament came the basilicas of the early centuries. In protest against the worldliness of the common churches a whole monastic movement arose, a movement that purified and preserved the Christian heritage after the fall of Rome. Hard upon the medieval period came the reaction of the Reformation, with vernacular worship, the simpler Eucharist, and even major services of the Word without the Lord's Supper, the Sacrament being celebrated but once or twice a year. On the left wing of the Reformation, sects such as the Quakers arose. Two centuries later there were great lay movements such as the Y.M.C.A., the Salvation Army, and the mass evangelism and evangelical societies of the American frontier. New forms of our own century have included the campus ministry, the hospital chaplaincy, and the German academies.

One fact is certain about every enduring new form that arises: new creative movement is institutionalized. "Charisma" is "routinized," to use the language of the German scholar Max Weber. New forms become institutions, with possibilities of obstructing as well as serving the life of faith.

Many of the arguments against the church are based on false assumptions about what it is called to be. This book would argue its case by presenting a framework with which to understand the nature and mission of the existing local church. On this basis what goes on in the church can be criticized and modified from a coherent point of view.

Many different ways of understanding the church have been suggested, but often they have failed to provide a view wide enough to encompass all the valid activity manifest in the churches as they are.

If only a narrow view of the church's mission is proposed and much of the activity of the churches is left uninterpreted, churchmen are left in confusion. They know intuitively that there has been valid meaning in the old, rejected forms. Although they know the ambiguities in the church as it stands, they cannot leap to untried new forms by discarding familiar ones that have been a means of grace for them. Those who find the old forms dead can and must make that leap, and many significant patterns of experiment are arising for just that reason. But when a congregation with a meaningful pattern of worship and some sense of its mission of service, idolatrous though much of its life may have been, is called a "heretical form" of the church, any member of that congregation who has found in it a mediation of the word of God to him can properly object.[3]

Colin Williams reports with approval the application of such a term as "heretical forms" to the residential churches as "not fitted to express God's true relation to the present world." The point must be made that such language could be cynically used to damn every institution that attempts to serve in God's name. Williams does have worthy suggestions for new gatherings of Christians for effective mission, and concerned Christians will react with enthusiasm to these forms whether they arise within or beyond typical congregational life.

To illustrate the problem of unfortunately narrow statements of the purpose of the church, consider but two of them. These approaches appear to offer adequate ground for renewal, but they are too limited. They reduce the broad meaning of the church to a single variety of meaning. They do not reform the whole of church life; they discard important parts of it because they fail to interpret them within their reductionist view. To the simplistic challenge to renewal, our response still must be: the wider church is not expendable.

One example of a one-track definition of the church—that of the revivalist—would go like this: "We who believe have been given to know the redemptive activity of God in Jesus Christ. We erect our platforms and buildings simply to announce this good news to our fellowmen."

If we discount the danger of pride in such a formulation, we can see the usefulness of this approach. From it some valid critical questions about our church activity follow: "Do we really proclaim good news with what goes on in our churches? Shall we not end our internal activities and concentrate our energies on public evangelism?"

Other aspects of church program can be interpreted and shaped according to this central theme. "We should vastly expand our use of public media," might be one implication. "We must attract attention and gain hearers for the message; use the press, the radio, and television." "We should consider using more billboards." "We must design imposing buildings at major public places to give witness to God's saving work for men." The revivalist interprets services of worship primarily as meetings for emotion and for preaching in which newcomers hear the invitation of the gospel and others reaffirm it more and more.

Such a single-minded approach a committed churchman can understand. Much of what is chaff in church activity is judged by it. Aggressive in its sense of mission, the view does not tolerate complacency. But real communication of a message is not so simple as billboards and revival meetings. And the traditions of the church which are left out of this perspective cannot be so easily discarded—the liturgical understanding of worship as more than preaching and emotion, the concrete action of the church as a force in the world to serve the needs of men in their social order. The preaching Christ may be lifted up by revivalism, but not the servant Lord.

Another one-track definition of the church takes quite another tack. It treats the church almost exclusively as a community engaged in "servanthood"—social service and social reform. In this era of social change we are likely to hear the statement, "If any organization ought to be right out front in the struggle for civil rights, it is the church." (And we can thank God that major parts of the movement have been very much church-related, in the person of the late Martin Luther King, Jr., and the hundreds of churchmen behind him.) By the same token we could go on, however: "If any group ought to be fighting on the front lines in the war on poverty, in helping individuals who are lost in mass culture, in battling mental illness, in caring for the aged, in strengthening the UN, it ought to be the church."

If the church is seen as the totality of its members in all their activities—and that is one important way of understanding the church—then this is true. It is also true that the church as an institution needs to develop a stronger voice in many directions such as these.

To take this approach exclusively, however, is to stop with too narrow an interpretation of the significance of the church. The approach lays aside a great sector of activity that has characterized the church throughout its history: namely, worship and prayer. It defines the church in such a way as to leave it undifferentiated from many other types of social and political activity; thereby the church seems essentially to be dismissed, even if for very humane reasons. "Wherever there is reconciliation among a group of people, the church happens," says this point of view. Therefore, forget the "religious" marks and let us get men reconciled one to another. Such a position is little help in defining the nature of the church, for church-men are hardly the only men who love their neighbors. The danger of the definition is that with all-out investment in social service, we unnecessarily risk forgetting the truth and power of religious undergirding for the ultimate norm of neighbor love itself.

No, the church is not expendable. We need a broad definition to say what is the church and what its unique function is. Only then dare we begin to review its shape and substance for a changing time like ours. For such a definition, we cannot stop with a single phrase from Scripture, ignoring the centuries that have elapsed since it was written (for example, the revivalist's "proclaim the gospel"). Neither can we take some well-meaning but contemporary definition that ignores all past religious experience.

In Chapters Two and Three, after briefly clearing some ground and surveying some resources on which we can build, we will review a systematic theory of the function of the church. That statement will then serve as a tool for evaluation and guidance for a discussion of the typical activities of the local church with a view toward their renewal.

Chapter Two

CLEARING THE GROUND
AND LAYING FOUNDATIONS

In order to erect a building on a wooded lot, we first clear space for the foundations. One valuable step toward understanding the nature and necessity of the local church is to clear a space by opening a way where certain criticisms of the church seem to impede us. We will learn from listening to the critics, however, and our building should be the better for it.

One form of criticism we face is a claim that men are inoculated by little doses of religion until they are immune to catching the real thing. Put in stronger words, critics suggest that the churches in their present form prevent us from a genuine encounter with the world into which we are born, and it is through just that encounter that men meet the God who creates and redeems them. If the church is isolated from existence, it forms a spiritually unhealthy retreat. It is Peter Berger's thesis in *The Noise of Solemn Assemblies* that the use most Americans make of the church, the function it serves for them, is as a retreat because of its irrelevance to life in the world.[4]

True Christian faith is the deep awareness of our ultimate need of God and his grace and a trustful loyalty and obedience to him. Mere respectable churchgoing is of course no such thing in itself. Churchgoing may be only the discovery of comfort in what passes for religion without any such commitment whatever.

Therefore, say the critics, the wrong kind of churchgoing can keep men happy enough that they do not open their lives to the experience of despair, the confession of sin, or the discovery of joy in the throbbing pulse of a more vital and useful life.

We must concede that many people are inoculated against deep emotional experience by routine substitutes for it. They may move through life only a little uneasy, using their church for a crutch to support their self-confidence but never truly confessing to God their weakness, never knowing his forgiveness. These people feel better for their participation in worship and in the fellowship of the church, but they are not healed. Seeing this, some critics argue as follows: To learn the true dimensions of human misery and the grandeur of God's grace, get away from the church. The church serves the wrong purpose. As Berger puts the case: "Religion provides the individual with the means by which he can hide from himself the true nature of his existence. . . . In a word, religion prevents ecstasy. It prevents the individual from stepping outside the routine of his everyday life in society and looking at himself in freedom. . . . The social irrelevance of the religious establishment is its functionality."[5] Popular religiosity is an inocuous faith in faith rather than a faith in God. The critic says that the God of this popular religiosity is dead and he ought to be. The forms taken by the piety that worships him tend to be religiously meaningless and as such they harm us because they pass for religious faith itself.

At the time of the first clamor criticizing the United States Supreme Court for its decision in the Regents' prayer case, one sane commentator supported the decision in the following way. He suggested that the children of serious-minded Christian and Jewish parents were certainly not harmed by the decision, for their nurture in the home was sound enough. Nor, he added, were the children of wholly secularized or atheistic families hurt, for such an exercise would not do anything for them either, and it might well make for ridicule of an empty religious form. He went on to say that those who stood to lose as they saw it were the parents who wanted the forms of religion observed without the content. They were those who were not religiously committed to the extent that their home life and their church life taught their children to pray. Therefore they hoped for some semblance of prayer in the public school. Here again, implied the critic, was a picture of inoculation: If children praying in school and not in church should believe themselves to be sharing in a living tradition of religious faith, they were deceived. Somewhat the same thing can happen inside the church, says the "inoculation" critic of the present church.

The mistake within the view that the church inoculates with its weak religion is the familiar "all-or-none" fallacy. Either you are on my side or you are subversive. Either faith means to you a radical break from the values of society or it is not religious faith at all.

There is Biblical justification to be found for this position if we look to the hard commands of Jesus or the words of the prophets by themselves. But direct application of these words to the complexities of human life results in a counsel of perfection which would prevent every morally sensitive man from claiming religious faith. The gospel condemns man's pride in his religion. Jesus calls the Pharisees "whitewashed tombs." But to say that every plain man who finds meaning enough in religion to attend church is inoculated against true faith because he is not yet a saint is to jump to the wrong conclusions. He may be on the way to faith, on the way from milk of babes toward solid meat, to use a metaphor from Paul.

A second form of criticism of our churches is that they represent not primarily religious faith but sociability in religious guise. This too would be a perversion of the Christian faith if it were the whole story. Churches that are mere clubs in religious masquerade should be disbanded.

The impressive growth of church membership in the '50s was to a large extent the result of a mammoth suburban migration of Americans. Suburbia grew for several reasons. Now that housing was available, families left off doubling up, and married couples set out to their own households, leaving the original family residence for their parents. A backlog of housing need was met and urbanization advanced at a rapid pace. From both the rural areas and the central cities, young families poured into the suburbs.[6]

In their new homes Americans wanted to belong, and in the new suburbs there were few ready-made organizations and institutions for belonging—except the church and the school. This was the decade of the P.T.A. and the church couples clubs. It was a decade when new families sought roots for lives made almost migratory by patterns of employment and the trade-in style of home ownership. The typical period of residence in many a suburban home was but three years. William H. Whyte, Jr., documented this startling suburban family pattern in *The Organization Man.* The thesis that these migrants wanted identity, not merely as Americans but as Americans of one of the three faith groups, is brilliantly outlined by Will Herberg in *Protestant—Catholic—Jew.* In the booming '50s all major denominations were planning new churches for the suburbs, programming church schools, and spawning couples clubs.

It is significant to note the new importance of the schools in this American suburbia. Whole communities revolved around the schools; the pattern is well described in a study of a Toronto suburb, *Crestwood Heights.*[7] In the medieval town, life centered on the church and the ceremonials in its plaza. Today's suburban communities often have little center except the school and its busy P.T.A., unless an active "community" church is established.

Inherent in these young and bustling churches, by the very fact of their rapid growth, was the danger of shallow religiosity. The churches were serving very real human needs. At least those persons of a gregarious bent were helped immensely with the settling-in process. There was not, however, any necessary correlation of growth in numbers with religious maturation. One might suggest that sociability is implied by the Christian teaching of the love of neighbor. However, the very chumminess of the brotherhoods and of the couples clubs often resulted in ingrown churches that stand aloof from and are even hostile to a consideration of the problems of more distant neighbors in the racial ghettos or the economically handicapped areas of the central city. These churches, serving a limited human need in the suburban community, are idolatrous in turning deaf ears to needs beyond their own neighborhood.

What are we to conclude from such a critical picture of the church? Shall we simply write across it the word "betrayal" and dismiss those churches where ingrown fellowship is king? Or shall we write more gently, "falls short"? If we find betrayal that is irreversible, we must do battle against the churches— destructive battle. If we find weakness, then we may work with what we have, accepting recent years—as we do previous centuries of church history—as a gift in the providence of God. We will work critically, but constructively, and always in fear and trembling—for, as Barth says, "we are fully aware of the eternal opposition between the Gospel and the church."[8]

Both answers have been given by critics of the churches. Radical revision is necessary, say some, marking off great sectors of the church as ineffective and irredeemable in their present, popular parish-church forms. Some see no way at all in which the church can be a mass movement. It is bound to be only a faithful remnant, so stringent are the demands of the gospel. With their large membership and watered-down requirements, their fairs and bazaars, their sales-world tactics of money-raising and their platitudinous sermons, the churches have betrayed Christian faith. We would be better off, it is implied, with a return to a narrow sect-consciousness which would close up these temples of mammon and call out of the world and into the church only the highly disciplined and faithful few.

We can learn from such a position our need for a heightened self-consciousness of our vocation as a disciplined people of God. That we can also learn from the sects. Ideally the church is a community rooted in common belief and moral discipline rather than one more voluntary association organized, in this case, around a steeple.

The position, however, also implies—and wrongly—that a pure church can exist, one not under the judgments that the broad church suffers. The gospel stands over and against the sect group as it does over and against the broad church. The tension to which the words of the Gospel point when Jesus says, "I have not come to bring peace, but a sword," is not solely the tension between church and world. It is a tension within— between the old man and the new man in everyman. Problems of hostility, rebellion, and personality distortion arise as readily within the sect and the utopian community as they do outside it.

Again the position forgets the use that God makes of very human and "worldly" processes. We cannot often separate the social process in the church from that process by which men learn that they belong to a community of faith. We can't easily separate the security a child learns through the loving care of his parents from that which he learns in the love of God. The two processes are not identical in either case, but they intermingle in such a way that one comes about by means of the other. Depending on what presuppositions we begin with, we may see more of one or the other or perhaps none of the other at all. "We have this treasure in earthen vessels."[9]

The work of ministry in the midst of the growth in the past decade and a half has been both exhilarating and exhausting. Pastors and lay leaders have had a hard time simply keeping up with the numbers in many new suburban churches. Therefore, unless we are simply to write off these churches altogether, the crucial task at present is to transform parish life until it feeds the hungers of men that lie deeper than the mere need to belong. Such is the guidance given us by the criticism which claims that churches have been captive to mere sociability. The rootedness that men need is more than human fellowship. It is ultimately the grace of God.

It is the purpose of this book to suggest what a Christian congregation most essentially can and ought to be so that all the diverse activities of a church can be molded by the central purpose for which they exist. The church is called to serve human need, but human need is far-ranging. Homes and farms, banks and bedsteads all serve human need. The church could spend its energy in providing family recreation or in organizing breadlines for the poor, in promoting thrift or in building furniture and it would still be meeting human need. Our question is about the unique function of the church, a question discussed in Chapter Three.

The thrust of the argument thus far is the assertion that the local churches have certain resources which are not to be written off either because some men wrongly think their church-going is the same as deep-going faith or because the churches often serve merely social ends. These resources can now be catalogued.

1. High among the assets of the church today is the fact that a large number of people are related to congregations. This is an extremely ambiguous asset. False concern for harmonious relations among large memberships is a millstone preventing many churches from properly taking up their work of mission. Literally thousands of churches would be stronger if they were to lose a third or even half their membership because their work and witness had become incisive enough—on the race issue, for example, or on the need for suburb and inner city to work together—to offend the "dead wood" on the membership lists. In balance, they would be stronger in ways that count the most.

Nevertheless, in general the large number of churchgoers is to be reckoned an asset. Even for those who are in church simply because of the need to "belong," there is a meaning to the church that is not lightly to be dismissed. One layman said very simply, and actually with profound meaning implicit in his comment, "The church is what gives me roots and tells me where I am." Religion has always been a corporate and communal affair, and so long as there is in the congregation a more articulate core who know more explicitly the source of faith and faith's claim of a loyalty above the culture, it is not necessary to disband the congregations which have arisen in this period of broad churchmanship in order for renewal to take place. Rather will we work to make of the multiform participation in church activity an expression of commitment to the meaningful center of the church's life.

Martin Marty, in contrast to more negative critics, is right when he says of this positive approach to the fact of widespread religious participation in our country, "We already possess the institutions we need to undertake the religious task set before America today." He admits, "They must be revised; they must grow; they need to be purged."[10] But, he says, our best hope is not in their replacement by other forms of the church.

We can and must affirm the churches in spite of all their ambiguities. Paul Tillich, writing of the church at the end of his major theological work, takes full cognizance of these ambiguities. Nevertheless, he states his conviction and hope: "There is regenerative power in the churches, even in their most miserable state."[11]

Such convictions are born of knowledge of the church's history, in which renewal has taken place repeatedly. They are born from appreciation of the fact that the church worships toward signs of God's presence in the world—the Cross, the Word, the Table—and that there is therefore an openness to new life. They are born of faith in a living God who can use even weakness to his own ends.

2. A second asset is the current ferment for new forms of church mission to supplement the typical local church. Providing feedback to the local church is one of the major functions of new forms. These ministries can serve as "scouts" to help the church understand the world from vantage points unavailable to most local churches. They help the church listen in the way the prophets did—looking around at the world to see what God seems to be saying to the ones who claim to be his people. The new structures or task groups can serve the research and development function which must be performed in any effective institution in a changing society, and their experimentation can give the church new life in worship, education, and social action. They may do very important work that most local churches by their very nature cannot do. Before long it is quite possible that 50 percent of the churches' professionally trained personnel will be involved in leadership other than that of the typical parish minister.

One example of what is meant by new forms and the need for them can be cited to illustrate this reference to supplemental forms of church mission. One of the most striking problems for the relevance of the church in modern society is its distance from the world of work. Traditionally the basis of a congregation has been the residental neighborhood. But today the residential church often becomes largely a church for women and children because they are the ones whose lives are primarily centered in the neighborhood. Even their lives move far beyond it—to the shopping center miles away; to recreation at a beach, amusement park, or summer cottage; to school by bus. These activities take them outside the neighborhood frequently. But think of the men. Daily their lives are committed to their work, and their work almost universally lies far outside the neighborhood. The chief personal identity of a breadwinner of the managerial and professional class is not his family but his work. For most men, "place" in society comes through occupation. Geographically and symbolically, the church for the man seems peripheral, a leisure-time and family-related activity far from many of the concerns closest to his understanding of his own life.

It is commonplace to say that the decisions men make in society ought to be guided by religious and ethical insight, that "religion is related to all of life." But only activity outside the typical residential parish will effectively help this come to pass. How is reflection upon God's will related to the allocation of natural resources in corporate and governmental offices, to the patterns on the drawing boards of the city planners, to the emphases in educational content and method? What does it have to say about the programming on TV and the content in the press? Where is this concern in the midst of industry, in which competitive posture, personnel policy, and labor relations so affect the lives of individuals and whole communities? All these activities involve moral decisions which will come from the most fundamental assumptions of the men involved. How can the churches take their proper role alongside these processes?

It is quite fair to say that many of the men involved in such important activity really "live" at work and only sleep in their houses. They do even that rarely enough, some sales and executive "widows" will say. Yet the churches have been neighborhood based. There is a need for new ways in which the churches can relate to the work of men and to the decision-making centers of our culture.[12] "Industrial missions" and other new forms of church mission are developing for just this reason, and they constitute a major resource for enlarging the vision of local churches.

Besides clearing the space, a builder must lay out foundation lines with the proper orientation. In defining the function of the religious enterprise in the life of men we can easily be misled.

First, we must not begin by saying, as some laymen on Every Member Canvass Sunday are tempted to do, that the church is a good thing to have around because it is an agency of community service. As such it often fails or is outdone by Junior Leagues and Boy Scouts and the United Fund.

This is not to suggest that the church should not be deeply involved in community service. But community service is not the essence of the church. If it were, we could raise many strange questions about the program of the church. Why the services on Sunday? Why the Bible education rather than sociology and psychology? Why the church school—can't the public schools do the job more effectively?

Secondly, we shall not begin by saying that the church is a legacy from the past and should be kept alive for its historical significance. One student contemplating the ministry could express himself only in this way. He came from a church with strong traditional emphasis and he kept repeating that it would be a tragedy for this church to die out. Of course he had an inarticulate sense of something meaningful in the historical rootage of the church. This history is *not* bunk. That our fathers believed is worthy of our reflection whether we can believe or not. But many old patterns of life have had to die—feudalism, cottage industry, slavery. Tradition alone cannot justify the church. Nostalgia is no basis for a call into the church's service either as minister or as layman.

Thirdly, the church might be defended as a custodian of morality, as if no other way could be found to keep men moral than by speaking of God and his moral law. Whether God exists or not, this view would seem to say, we need to speak of him as the grounding for morality. People won't be good without it. Keep religion alive, and put "moral and spiritual values" into our schools where possible. These twin instruments will sustain our society. The church is a good thing.

Certainly Christian faith has been a major source of morality for men and it has been justified by many of its defenders as the bulwark of a sane and moral society. However, this is not the way one goes about challenging men to trust one's word—"It seems a good thing so let's pretend it's true. Whether we believe in God, or not, let's speak of him because it will help our children to be good."

For a fourth example, consider the "patriotic" fallacy, used in defense of the church. There has been a period, not yet slipping into the past, when we could hear men urging church attendance and church support for the sake of American strength and American character. This kind of argument is a summons to Americanism, to democracy, and to the American "way of life," with the church as a prop valued for its utility. It is not a summons to trust and obedience toward the God who is above the nation and whom we *may* serve or *may not* serve in our patriotism, depending upon its nature. There is little in this argument in common with the Biblical faith in a God who says, "My thoughts are not your thoughts, neither are your ways my ways." If the American way of life appears to demand something other than belief in God and participation in churches, then, following this utilitarian argument, the church becomes expendable.

If the church is what it claims to be, an instrument of the divine will, the question may be asked the other way around with considerable justification: How has America contributed to the truest life of the church? How has the nation served God's purpose for man? How has it failed to do so? These are the ultimate questions addressed to the churches and all the other institutions of American society. To defend God and the religious institution for the contributions they make to culture is to make the culture the chief value and, therefore, an idol. This is to defend an alien god which is not God. This is to reject God and leave him behind as dead.

The hazards of such a line of argument are found in the development of the "German Christians" during the early years of Hitler's Third Reich. The church that looks to culture for its justification will betray God when the culture does. Only by understanding its own reality in obedience to God can it remain a true church. In the German case, the changing culture, following the advent of Hitler, asked changes in the churches that could not be easily resisted. But the Confessing Christians who resisted the influences of German nationalism in the churches declared in the great Barmen meeting of 1934: "Jesus Christ ... is the one Word of God which we have to hear and which we have to trust and obey in life and in death." There was to be no acknowledgment of a lordship of Hitler or German culture alongside. This was the beginning of martyrdom and exile and the Resistance, a great twentieth-century chapter of church history. With all the values of American life and the political system we have, there must be vigilant care that in the ways we think of the Christian faith we are not seduced into becoming American Christians as there were German Christians.

We believe that the church is here by God's will to serve him in the ministry of reconciliation, the ministry of bringing together, beyond their estrangement, man and God. If it is implicit in that statement that the institutional church engage in social service, maintain a tradition, teach morality, and serve the nation, well and good. If it is not, then the church must obey God rather than men.

In a sense, the church is an article of faith. "I believe in ... the holy catholic church." So runs the creed. As we argue that the church is not expendable, we begin with the Credo, the "I believe," which looks toward God. Then we define the necessary place of the church in a view of man that knows him as a child of God. The Christian faith speaks of man always as man-before-God. It does not know man-on-his-own first and build from there.

We believe in the church because we believe in God. We believe the church is purposefully here by God's grace and that these clusters of believers and half-believers scattered through the cities and countryside are "earthen vessels" to show forth a transcendent power that belongs to God. The churches are voluntary associations, sociologically speaking, just as the Boy Scouts and the Y.M.C.A. and the Masonic lodges. But they make a unique claim. They participate in a sacred history through which God in a particular way is working his will for men in the world, forgiving sinners, calling men to himself.

The church is a human institution and therefore it is full of all the distortions that humanity carries wherever it goes. But beyond, within, through the institution there is this other meaning: the church is God's.

There is a double vision necessary to understand the church. The eyes of faith see it as a God-given instrument for God's purposes, one that exists within the categories of time and space, of group dynamics and social class, of town and countryside and city. They must also see it as a fallen thing, betraying and denying God's will because of men's prideful behavior in the forms of caste and class, of psychological manipulation and anxiety, of exploitative authority and power.

The most familiar New Testament metaphor used of the church calls it the body of Christ. The metaphor helps us in several ways. In the Christian doctrine of the Incarnation, we interpret the meaning of a fully human life, that of Jesus of Nazareth. Here was a carpenter's son born and raised and finally put to death in an obscure part of the Middle East at a time when most "important" history was taking place in Rome. Likewise, in calling the church the body of Christ, we interpret the significance of a full human institution. The church includes groups of all manner of description by denomination and practice, powerless and rather obscure to nearsighted estimates of the powers that shape the history of mankind and the private lives of men. Faith knows greater meaning than meets this nearsighted eye.

Thus "body of Christ" implies an embodying of the will and word of God in the concrete and day-by-day created world. If God is transcendent, the Incarnation says also that he moves within history to reveal himself. He does not leave himself without voice, without form in the substantial historical world.

Christianity is a materialism—dealing with the realities of

life in the here and now. It does not retreat in an escapist spiritualism which dismisses present realities. Rather, Christianity claims that God invades time. He invades the time which is already his time because it is his creation. He gives himself in the divine self-giving of the cross. The fulfillment of creation is a man wholly open to God and wholly self-giving for his fellowmen. This fulfillment is actualized within space and time. So great is God's acceptance of finitude in the created world that the Jesus of the Gospels comes in the meekness of Bethlehem's stable and lives incognito until his disciples begin to call him Messiah.

So too may we see God's man-relatedness in the church. The church becomes part of his covenant with man, an instrument of his. The church must think of itself as part of God's revelation of himself, part of his self-giving in the world. We bear this divine command to be the body of Christ in the world. The implications are many. Not the least of them is the probability that the body of Christ must suffer in self-giving also. There may be an incognito quality to much of our service; it asks no recognition. These are our marching orders if we but realize who we are as part of the body. We are called to all this in spite of the inevitable fallibility of the churches as human institutions.

This is the paradox of the church: "The church dissolves the gospel, the gospel the church." But there is nowhere else for the Christian to be than in the church in its broadest sense. The attempt at reconciling man and God must be made. The church must be formed among men. That designated as the body of Christ must live in confession and hope among the lively affairs of men. To the eyes of faith, God ordains the church to its mission.

Chapter Three

WHAT IS GOING ON HERE?

When a group of people call themselves a church, what really is going on? Ask them and they will answer many different things: "We are praising God." "We are teaching our children the faith of their fathers." "We solemnize marriages and bury the dead." "We serve the community." Some members of the group will have no answer save to say that people "just ought to belong to a church."

Social scientists can look at the church and, without reference to faith, see certain processes taking place. "Religious participants strengthen their sense of social solidarity," they will say. "They affirm personal identity as Protestants, Catholics, or Jews." "They strengthen the bonds of marriage; they reaffirm life in the presence of death." "They teach discipline and religious law to the younger generation." "They satisfy personal ego; they feel important by virtue of charitable deeds and officeholding in the church."

Theologians look at the church with another judgment. They can say this same group gathers in the name of Christ for the purpose of proclaiming the gospel and serving men in Christ's name. If it does not, it ought to. All that is done should serve this Christian end.

Actually both social scientists and theologians, within their own proper limits, can be right. It is helpful to keep both approaches in mind as we formulate an answer to the question that heads this chapter. In our fast-changing and increasingly secularized society the church is suffering something of an identity crisis. Its members ask, "Just who are we as a gathered group?" Any realistic understanding of the church today must comprehend both the social and the theological dimensions of its life. The challenge is to tie the two dimensions together into one clear statement. These are times when a mere proof text from the New Testament ("You are the body of Christ") does not communicate to all churchmen enough of an answer to the identity crisis of the church.

One negative statement can make way for a positive step toward defining what the church most essentially is and does. In the church we are not in the business of winning the blessing of God or manipulating the gift of faith. Christian faith cannot be guaranteed to a man by anything the church can do. This is one of the most basic of all our Christian tenets. Prophetic religion has continually attacked the religious institution for priestly arrogance when it assumed that men could curry God's favor through religious forms. New Testament Christianity exploded across the Roman Empire with just such a realization: "While we were yet sinners Christ died for us." This experience provides a norm that separates Christian faith from all systems for propitiating the gods or for ceremonial manipulation to control the Deity.

Thus Christian faith appears at first to deny validity to the very institution we seek to understand. From the narrative about the tower of Babel to the parable of the Pharisee and the publican told by Jesus, Scripture implies that the religious institution is almost more likely to stand as a barrier to God's way with man than as an avenue to serve it. Religion becomes proud. Modern men understand this very well and that understanding intensifies the identity crisis of the church. In Søren Kierkegaard's biting *Attack on Christendom,* as in contemporary writers such as Peter Berger and Gabriel Vahanian, the "religious establishment" and our present "religiosity" are seen as forms of irreligion and unfaith. Man looks around for "religionless Christianity."

What positive statement is to be made about the church's essential function? Granted that the God-relation is nothing we create and that the institution may be perverse, what is left to us as a way of understanding church activity? The church is an embodiment of faith. Faith drives toward expression. Some explicit form is needed to proclaim the central fact that human life exists in the context of God's grace. The expression assists men adequately to know who they are and what their lives are about. When men and their cultures remain unaware of the God-relation they suffer a crucial deprivation. In short, Christian faith must take on flesh.

This "enfleshment" serves two functions from the point of view of the Christian community. One is internal, one external. Internally, we give shape to faith for the sake of self-understanding, both as individuals and as a community. We celebrate who we are, most commonly at worship, but in just as real a way in deeds of service. Both worship and social action feed back a greater sense of identity for the Christian community.

Sometimes as a man wrestles with a very serious decision, he steps aside to write columns marked "pro" and "con" or even a paragraph stating as explicitly as possible what his major life goals are, "who he is." Our celebration of the God-relation at worship and in other avenues of church life clarifies faith in a similar way. People may "enjoy" worship or "feel better" after having been to church, but it is not necessary that they do. The basic function being served is the restatement for the individual and the group of their fundamental identity: man-before-God.

In one area in India a new Christian is taught that upon rising in the morning he should place a hand on his head in memory of his baptism and say simply, "I am a Christian." This simple ritual does not constitute Christian faith; yet as a response of faith, it helps sustain Christian identity.

Secondly, religious activity has an outward direction to it. Forms and institutions are necessary if the church is to "proclaim the gospel" or to "set at liberty those who are oppressed." The church helps the whole culture move toward a life-style appropriate to the fact that the world exists not by some chance quirk of the cosmos but by the providence of God.

Christian faith must take on flesh. There is a uniquely Christian reason for saying this about the way we understand the importance of a religious institution. Augustine long ago said he had already found in the philosophers many of the things Christians had been trying to teach him, but one thing he did not find—that "the Word became flesh and dwelt among us." In its doctrine, Christianity is a daringly materialistic religion. In the Incarnation, God himself chooses an explicit form of activity quite opposed to mere revelation of general principles. He comes to man in the person of Jesus Christ. The person or community that professes Christian faith likewise gives form to its faith, takes a definite place in the history of the world around it. There is that commission: "You are the body of Christ."

A man who trusts God moves inevitably toward expressing his faith in worship and in neighbor love. As it is explicitly enacted and defined, faith gains greater clarity or more importance as a central theme in man's life. We dare not say dogmatically that the man lacks faith who neither worships nor reaches out in external deeds of love. He may lie on his deathbed with an internal courage or confidence that no other man knows. As a "happy pagan" he may simply make life brighter wherever he is present. But the drive toward articulation is a theme of Scripture and a constant of man's own experience. The psalms are rooted in the desire to sing praise or to express to God confession or complaint. The word of the Lord was a "burning fire . . . in my bones," said Jeremiah, and he had to speak it (Jer. 20:9). The apostles said they could not but speak the things they had heard and seen (Acts 4:20). Paul said, "Woe to me if I do not preach the gospel" (I Cor. 9:16). And Luke spoke it, too, when he wrote out the Palm Sunday narrative: "I tell you that, if these should hold their peace, the stones would immediately cry out" (Luke 19:40).

Christian faith must take on flesh. Consider two analogies that help enlarge upon this theme.

One analogy is from the arts. The artist is not merely a person who senses beauty. He is one who gives expression to his aesthetic sensitivity. The writer is only a restless, latent poet until he actually expresses the words buried in the recesses of his mind or only potentially manifest in the depths of his emotions. Had he written nothing else, Goethe could not be called a poet during the sixty years that Faust lived only within him, unarticulated. The artist becomes artist through his work; he is no artist until he creates the sonnet or symphony or sculpture. Similarly, subtle and varied as the forms of it may be, some kind of expression is necessary to Christian existence.

The other analogy is from marriage. It illustrates the manifold ways in which we may give expression to religious faith. By saying that religion is the articulation of faith, we risk implying that this is a merely verbal or intellectual affair. But think how marriage expresses itself. For a man and wife, the relation of faithfulness and trust may rarely take shape in the words "I love you." The words can be spoken too much just as they can be spoken too little. Similarly the sexual relation of itself does not constitute marriage. But there must be form, and the right use of many forms constitutes marriage—spoken words, cooperative homemaking, leisure activity, simple companionship, sexual union—all serve to actualize and deepen the marriage relation.

Other external factors contribute. There is the legal contract, signifying societal expectations and requirements; there is the physical place—a house or apartment, with the society of friends and strangers identifying this place as the home of Mr. and Mrs. Smith or Schmidt or Kazakian. If there is a child, he irrevocably is the child of this father and this mother in spite of divorce or separation. Internally, there are memories shared by this man and this woman, and there are common hopes. That couple is blessed who can speak these things in words. But far more than words make a marriage. Similarly, activities far beyond mere words help constitute the people of God and serve to give form to faith.

The idea that we must embody faith is helpful in thinking through some knotty problems of religious practice. For example, there is the problem that the several elements of religious activity appear to go off in such different directions that they cancel each other. The churchman preoccupied with liturgy can forget or fail to understand the prophetic work that must be an integral activity of the Christian community. The evangelist may see worship solely as revival, and may think social action to be only incidental. The man of social passion may see little point in liturgy that does not explicitly exhort to moral action. If we think of the church as an expression of the God-relation, there is room for each man under this inclusive rubric, and there is ground for mediating the divergent claims they make upon the life of the church. As we come to define what the God-relation is, we will propose a relative perspective for each of these facets of the church's life.

Such an approach also helps us to understand the work of the congregation in a way that avoids placing the church and its members on a level of moral superiority to surrounding culture. Pride accompanying any understanding of the church, even if it derives from vigorous moral concern and self-discipline, is a distortion of the gospel. The life of the church itself is always ambiguous and fragmentary enough that the church dare not exalt itself above its culture. It does not possess norms with which to arbitrate all issues of social policy and cultural style. Just as we understand the many-members-one-body metaphor within the church, we also know the role of many institutions in the wider social fabric. Political, economic, and cultural endeavors are seen by Christians as God-given orders for the good of men. The work of those involved in these orders is not in any sense inferior to the religious work we do when we participate explicitly in the work of the church as an institution. The church is simply chartered to perform one function that must be served among men, the explicit expression of the Godward dimension of human life. That function is served by all those people who choose to or are moved to become the church.

This is quite a different view of church membership from that of many Christians, even now. Thus, as Martin Thornton says, confirmation is not an emotional experience but initiation to a job.[13] A person chooses to participate in the church so as to make explicit in human life the dimension of Christian faith. Thornton's statement is a strong one. This job in the church, he says, "has no peculiar interest in recruitment."[14] "Conversion is simply the vocational experience of desiring membership of the laity by baptism, just as vocation in a narrower sense is the same experience of desiring ordination. . . . Any static view of conversion as expressed by such a phrase as 'I am saved,' becomes self-condemned."[15]

Such a view cannot for a moment consider as beyond the grace of God those who are "outside" the churches. It cannot look down upon those who are not verbally professing Christians, and those who love and serve their fellowmen without religious self-consciousness. Since Vatican II even Roman Catholicism, which has been much more hesitant in this regard than liberal Protestantism, is more ready to talk about the "saving" grace of Christ which is effective for those who do not receive it through the church or explicitly acknowledge Christian faith. On the other hand, the principle that faith needs to be embodied does suggest the error of any sentiment that every man of goodwill is living the full Christian life. Nothing is more urgent for man than genuinely to know that "the earth is the Lord's . . . , the world and those who dwell therein." If such knowledge is served by religious embodiment of some sort, one essential dimension of responsible Christian life would appear to be a meaningful relationship to the church.

Jesus, in his summary of the law, says a man is to love God and love his neighbor. This double direction to our Christian task, the "vertical" and "horizontal," is symbolized also in the Ten Commandments. There, "religious" duties such as keeping the Sabbath are listed before the obligations toward one's fellowmen. However, the "second table" follows from the first without a break, and to the original Israelite there was no distinction. Justice for the neighbor is honor to God just as the Sabbath is. Conversely, sustaining among men a meaningful expression of the God-relation is part and parcel of the Christian's neighbor love. Karl Barth, in his massive *Church Dogmatics,* begins a volume on ethics with sections on the Sabbath and on prayer!

The calling of the church may be illustrated by the Biblical image of the Remnant, the group called out from among the whole. In the Bible, the Remnant refers to the faithful who are left as others bow down in idolatry. Because of its judgmental connotations, there is risk in the image. But the Remnant metaphor is based on the Hebrew consciousness of election to a particular covenantal bond and a particular function among the nations. God calls Israel ultimately for a saving purpose among surrounding peoples. With this functional meaning the term is a good one. This consciousness of Remnant-servanthood marks both Hebrew and Christian history, and it underlies the drive in Christian missions. The Remnant is called by God to faithfulness in showing forth his nature and will to the world, to the "Gentiles." It is a call to service and to vicarious suffering and not to any "lording over" others.

This is an awesome vocation for the people of God. The Remnant in Israel can be seen as suffering a progressive diminution until there is at last but One who is the faithful servant, suffering on a cross at Golgotha. Here is a sober warning of the cost that may be involved in the call to servanthood and Remnanthood.

This interpretation of the call of the church is expressed by Martin Thornton in these words: "The word Jesus used in speaking of his Body—the Church—is precisely that which in his native tongue means Remnant. 'Thou art Peter and upon this rock will I build my Remnant-Church.' . . . The religious life is vocational, it is the call to a job."[16] The religious life is what we elect with participation in worship and the other labors of the church, not for merit but because of its purpose in the providence of God and ultimately because we can do nought else. There is a fire in our bones. Recognizing the fact of our existence before God, we celebrate and rehearse the news of the gospel.

Many other Biblical images convey the same meaning of vocation for Christians and their churches. The church is to be salt, seasoning the earth, losing itself in dispersal among that which is to be seasoned, while disciplined enough to sustain its savor for the sake of the world. It is like leaven lost in the meal so as to leaven the whole lump.

Ultimately the nature of the relation between the form of faith and the substance of faith eludes us. We can fall erroneously to one side and say that faith depends on the forms we set up or require of men. We can fall to the other and leave faith spiritualized until it appears to lack reality altogether.

The subtlety of the relation may be illustrated by the nature of prayer. Abraham Joshua Heschel, the Jewish mystic-theologian, speaking of prayer, writes of the way we can say that explicit forms, such as the liturgy, feed faith while we cannot say they constitute faith. Heschel is speaking especially to the person who asks what use there is of written and spoken prayers if an individual is not "in the mood" for prayer. He is acknowledging that true prayer is far from being the same thing as speaking the words of prayer. But, he says,

What goes on between the soul of man and the word of prayer is more than an act of employment, of using words as if they were tools. Here the soul and the word react upon each other; the word is a creative force.

Most of us do not know the answer to one of the most important questions; namely, what is our ultimate concern? We do not know what to pray for. It is through the words of the liturgy that we discover what moves us unawares, what is urgent in our lives, what in us is related to the ultimate.

Why should we follow . . . the liturgy? Should we not say, one ought to pray when he is ready to pray? The time to pray is all the time. There is always opportunity to disclose the holy, but when we fail to seize it, there are definite moments in the liturgical order of our speech to remind us. These words are like mountain peaks pointing to the unfathomable. Ascending their trails we arrive at prayer.[17]

The ascent and arrival of which Heschel speaks could not happen unless there were the "experience" of prayer before and after many of the words of prayer. The words—the form, the articulation—are not identical with prayer. Faith does not consist in the form any more than God is dependent, in his relation to men, upon their churches and prayers. God is free. But the forms are used by God as instruments to give actuality to the prayer.

How essential is it that the church exist to give explicit form to this God-relation? What is the weakness of nonreligious life? By "nonreligious" we do not mean the great portion of any life that is carried on without direct relation to the religious institution. Rather we mean the life which has no coherence with a core of meaning that can be understood Christianly.

At one point Paul makes a radical judgment: "Whatever does not proceed from faith is sin" (Rom. 14:23b). Here is a startling interpretation of human life and the centrality of that Godward trust and loyalty and obedience which faith is. Everything, Paul says, that does not hang together around some meaningful center of ultimate concern is well understood as alienated from God. Therefore it is damned. This may seem a pessimistic view of life (actually it is far from it), but it corresponds to profound human experience. Lives not held together by some sense of identity, purpose, and destiny are likely to sour in the end. Work and leisure, marriage and public affairs can all move from meaningfulness to nausea and sin if they are not "saved" by this coherence.

For the Christian that center of meaning has been given. "The Word became flesh and dwelt among us, full of grace and truth." God's choice to be man-related "took shape" in the Incarnation in a unique way at the center of the long history of his explicit activity in the "salvation history" of Bible and church. The enfleshment of God is what the eyes of faith discover in Jesus, called, therefore, the Christ. Christ empties himself, says Paul (Phil. 2:1–11), taking the form of a servant, choosing the kind of reality that we know in flesh and blood. God will not remain "spiritual" only. He becomes historical. The Christian cannot accept a spiritualism as his religion— either the spiritualism of withdrawal from secular life into a "religious" one, or that opposite kind which says belief in God and humanitarian goodwill need no specifically religious shape in the economy of human life. If the church is called Christ's body, this is precisely one part of what is meant—that just as God makes his will known in the world through the man Jesus, one way his will is still made known is in the body of the church. The embodiment or articulation must still take place lest there be nothing in the midst of the world of men or in the life of an individual that points Godward so that it may then be discovered that God has opened life to his redemptive mercy. The church is not expendable.

Chapter Four

WHAT MEAN THESE STONES?

Suddenly, in the midst of public worship, many a churchgoer realizes he is terribly bored. He is neither learning, nor feeling, nor doing anything that seems significant. The whole procedure is for him as dead as last year's Christmas tree. He wonders whether it means more to any of those around him. Partly right, partly wrong, he is tempted to shout, "The emperor has no clothes."

Because of this common experience, and because worship is the single most distinctive mark of religious activity, we begin with worship in reflecting upon the meaning of parish life. Without any appreciation of worship, people justifiably drop their participation in it. Many of them return, discovering that there was meaning they had not understood. Many others do not, and whether this is good or bad may depend upon the other ways in which they live out the God-relation. Certain it is, however, that if nothing significant is taking place in worship, the church as we know it is a hollow shell and should be allowed to die. Worship remains the primary activity by which to identify the church; hence it provides the fundamental clue for understanding the church.

Formal public worship of itself does not constitute the church. So central is it, however, that the significance of Christian faith for most congregations rises and falls with the vitality of their corporate worship. That renewed understanding and vitality begin at this point is essential.

Why worship? Actually the question might be better put: How worship, and whom? All men in their most human moments use their lives in the service of some end or other. They attribute worth (worth-ship) to the purpose they serve and they give some interpretive form to this fact about their lives. In the broadest sense, they worship one god or another whether they ever come near a religious sanctuary. This "worship" may be relatively stylized, or it may be almost invisible.

Let us begin with a whimsical example, the collective sunbathing of early summer. Harmless as it is, we could view this ritual as a miniature liturgy in praise of leisure, the sun, and the physical body. That first bright day when the wide, warm beach opens its arms to receive the bathers, you often hear shouts of joy from men and women who have long suffered the gray, wintry sky. The first quick run out from the shadows and into the sun is a celebration, and celebration is probably the most helpful single metaphor with which to interpret Christian worship too.

More significant than sunbathing are political rallies which lift up a party loyalty and which proceed with a certain ceremonial format year after year. Celebration is here and, occasionally, confession. Both through rhetorical exhortation and through serious deliberation, the party expresses unity and a new level of dedication to common tasks. The whole mixture of hoopla and folksiness and backroom bargaining rehearses the political nature and necessity of man in community.

A man's worship may be an almost frantic pursuit of wealth, and his ritual an examination of bankbook and stock reports. For the music lover, it may be a regular pattern of attendance at the symphony, in part for pure enjoyment, but in part too, to lift up an ideal of the world of "culture." Only animals do not worship, neither bowing down before baalim nor putting their conscious strength toward any transcendent purposes. They do not celebrate or pledge allegiance, much as they are often bound together by strong group ties of herd or pack or colony. Man is not so much the animal who can make tools, or think, or govern himself, as he is the one who can pray.

Man's conscious nature drives him toward participation in life goals—the raising of children, the pursuit of pleasure, the building of corporations or kingdoms, the doing of good. Man finds an identity for himself from such pursuit. His sanity is sustained by the end he pursues, the structure of "last things" toward which he strives. The structure of his *telos* or purpose in turn is based on his ultimate hopes—those things he trusts and believes to be the end toward which his universe is moving.

Goals need not be socially or religiously approved to serve at least temporarily the emotional and mental functions of offering a man some sanity. The neurotic may find stability in a scheming drive for vengeance upon a partner whom he thinks to have wronged him. It is when such goals collapse or when there is internal contradiction in a given "faith" that the goals break down in their utility.

The Nazi movement provided a center for a certain kind of "sanity" in the recovery of the German economy and the national morale during the thirties. The ceremonials of the Hitler youth movement and the mass rallies of the Third Reich were furnished with a mythology and drama all their own. They served as a religion, a posture toward life, for their participants. They were defended as a remedy for the sickness of modern, "decadent," democratic man. The scheme worked, of course, only as long as the police state and self-deception could repress all questioning of the gods exalted by this "worship" and of the atrocities that followed from it. Because there had to be so much repression, this sanity was actually a form of psychosis, so out of touch with reality was the nation.

Every enduring culture develops collective articulation of its loyalties and aspirations. In the absence of bona fide religious worship on any meaningful scale, such alternatives as Hitler's rallies become a probability. Emile Durkheim propounded this view of the function of religion in society.[18] The French sociologist held that religious symbol and institution are totemic representations of the corporate welfare of the people. Therefore they are exalted and held inviolate. By this definition, fascism is clearly a religion. So too, in their own ways, are the communism of Red China and the ultra-Americanism of the radical right wing in our own country.

Is worship in the church but another form of the political rally or the concert hall? Hardly. In each case men are doing more than listening with rational minds—either to arguments about government policy or to musical harmonies and dissonance: they are collectively expressing a certain loyalty and celebrating a certain human capacity. In religious worship, however, an ultimate trust and loyalty is affirmed, and man rehearses his existence as a child of God.

Christian worship, seen from our human side of things,[19] is important for reasons not altogether unlike those which are manifest in the forms of political and cultural life. If, however, we believe that the most significant fact of our life is not the exaltation of leisure or politics or aesthetics, but rather, the fact of our God-relation, then it becomes necessary to articulate this dimension not merely as a parallel concern but as a basis for all the others. We give form to our pursuit of pleasure at the beach, to our political pursuits at the party convention, and to our aesthetic sense in the concert hall. Each activity can have a valuable and even a religiously meaningful place for us. However, rarely or only casually to articulate in an explicit way the ultimate context in which these activities take place is to leave our lives the poorer and far short of truth. As John Nevin put it in an important nineteenth-century plea for more depth in worship, "To be real, the human as such, and of course, the divine also in human form, must ever externalize its inward life."[20]

Worship is an explicit recognition of the God-relation. Even for the man who has not learned anything about liturgy, the mere fact of attendance at worship is not necessarily a meaningless exercise. It can be the articulation for him of this dimension of his selfhood, a punctuation mark for making some sense of the otherwise headlong rush of activity which may make up his life week after week.

Churchgoing can be misused, of course. It is as subject to exploitation for the wrong ends as any other pursuit. The shopkeeper may take profit legitimately as a return for service, or he may exploit the public in a monopolistic situation. Political

rallies and sexual relations can be good or bad, depending upon
their use. So too, worship can misrepresent and betray God's
reach for man. It may sustain a man in his pride, help him pretend to be what he is not, or find new customers. Properly it is
enactment of the God-relation in which our lives are set.

If articulating the God-relation is the task of worship, one
corollary follows easily: many different forms may serve this
function—all the way from the Catholic Mass to the Pentecostal
tent meeting. Cultural backgrounds will play a large part in
determining what is most meaningful for any group. There is
no eternally right and proper form.

Experimentation, a kind of "situation ethics" in worship, is
therefore justified. Jazz music and gospel song, Bach and
Vaughn Williams—all can be used in the church's worship on
occasion. We welcome novelty, however, for enlarging and
deepening worshipful expression, not for its publicity value. If
a jazz group sees its music as a lament to God or a shout of joy
to him, then their music is a possibility for the church. We can
mourn and rejoice with the group; they may speak for and with
the congregation engaged in worship.

Language and liturgy from an age gone by often mean little
to the man of today. We must not judge him to be religiously
tone-deaf on that account. The church owes him both new
patterns of worship and vigorous interpretation of its regular
style of liturgy. Liturgical renewal is not the unearthing of old
forms. It may include that, but much that is new can provide
a richer vehicle for modern man's celebration of who he is as
a child of God. Whenever the old is used it is used for a purpose, and this should be understood. The use of traditional
forms expresses the rootedness of men in the church through
time. It says that men are heirs of a history and members of
a vast "communion of saints."

While many forms can help us to enact our faith, what we
know of the God-and-man relationship helps shape our worship.
Thus, in the words of one scholar, whoever grabs the little fin-
ger of liturgy soon finds himself tugging at the whole fist of
doctrine. The shape of the liturgy should have determinants far

beyond the cultural preference of the participants. The Christian understanding of the God-relation is not that of the Buddhist, nor that of the Western humanist. Hence, widely varied as Christian forms have been, there are constants to be found in the church's worship and a few of these may now be examined.

One constant is the sense that God is personal and that men's relationship to him finds personal expression. Hence we address God in personal terms in the prayers of the church. In prayer we put into the form of words the fact and the possibility of personal response by men to the personal nature of God. In addressing God, therefore, we express the qualities of loyalty and trust, of hope and adoration that pertain to the personal relation. In confession we reveal ourselves to God. In the prayer of intercession we articulate before God the horizontal relationship of love. The Christian, as the Jew before him, has found God claiming and provoking his moral concern for the neighbor. In this context the believer finds himself inevitably expressing a concern for justice in the social order and for the welfare of "all sorts and conditions of men."

It takes only a little sophistication to raise deep questions about public prayer. Why speak words to God when "no secrets are hid" from him? Who is God that he is asked for this and that in petition and intercession? If there is regularity and autonomy in nature's law, and if there is human freedom, how can prayer be "effective"?

The first question to be asked, however, is not about the efficacy of prayer. Prayer's first function is not to get results, to "work." (The function of a celebration is not to get some kind of result—here again this metaphor helps us.) In prayer and in corporate acts of praise men put into form their sense of the God-relation. Prayer is the articulation of faith. One need not ask, "Does it work?" to begin to pray. He need ask only, "Who am I?" If the answer is, "I am a person, created by God for relationship to him," one is led to the inevitability of prayer of some sort. Man is restless, in this sense, until he finds his rest in prayer, in expression of his God-relatedness.

Certainly there are philosophical and psychological ways of discussing prayer. Paul Tillich, for example, is helpful in discussing intercessory prayer. After he has described God's relation to the created world as "directing creativity," he writes:

God's directing creativity is the answer to the question of the meaning of prayer, especially prayers of supplication and prayers of intercession. Neither type of prayer can mean that God is expected to acquiesce in interfering with existential conditions. Both mean that God is asked to direct the given situation toward fulfillment. The prayers are an element in this situation, a most powerful factor if they are true prayers. As an element in the situation a prayer is a condition of God's directing creativity, but the form of this creativity may be the complete rejection of the manifest content of the prayer. Nevertheless the prayer may have been heard according to its hidden content, which is the surrender of a fragment of existence to God. This hidden content is always decisive. It is the element in the situation which is used by God's directing creativity.[21]

Nevertheless, men pray most often without need for any rational analysis of their activity. Much simpler reflection than the above will also serve us well. One man may choose simply to say that by Scripture and tradition he is taught and commanded to pray, and let it rest at that. Another, reading anthropology, may think it clear that men have always prayed and will continue to do so, and so he prays as a whole man unencumbered by that rationalist skepticism which cannot see any sense in prayer.

The aesthetic analogy to religious observance helps us again in understanding prayer. The creative artist does not ask for his painting, sculpture, sonata, or poem, "What good will it do?" Rather, he finds himself both driven and freely choosing to give form to his sense of beauty or meaning. His choice of the medium for expression is dependent in part on his talent and in part on the inner conception itself. Indeed, the conception takes shape in his mind (and his whole nervous system) *by means of* the medium—form and color, musical line, verbal innuendo. Prayer serves an enabling function making for more profound awareness of our God-relation.

Play also may serve as an analogue to prayer and worship. One does not ask the purpose of play while engaged in it. Play is its own fulfillment. This would be a dour world indeed if play were valued only because it renewed man for work, making work the final end of life. Prayer and praise, like play, fulfill themselves. As the catechism put it, the chief end of man is "to glorify God and to enjoy him forever," a phrase which sounds like a definition of worship too.

Insisting on a test of strict utility can destroy more than prayer. Church architecture has a function that is more than housing a congregation. It too celebrates the God-relation, expressing, for example, joy or strength as a primary motif. Strict material utility is no final test of the church's ministry to human need. Men have nonmaterial needs as well. Even in social service, material tests fail. One can ask, "What good is it?" of the kindness lavished on a retarded "child" who is thirty-five years old, cared for in an institution, taught perhaps to sit up or read a short time before his death. Asking "usefulness" of these efforts is too shallow a request to deserve an answer. The church engages in social service for reasons of innate fulfillment and as natural expressions of faith quite similar to those of the artist, without always expecting much measurable social "good" to come of it.

A second constant that is expressed in worship is the self-revealing activity of God. God acts to claim man's loyalty, trust, and obedience. He speaks through the prophets and he "comes to man" in Jesus Christ. To Christians, one result of God's self-revealing activity is the Scriptural witness to his deeds through Israel and through Christ and the early church. Hence a regular part of worship is the use of Scripture. The reading of the Word, whether a single lesson or the multiple readings in more elaborate liturgies, is as much a celebration as it is the communication of content. The lesson is not a "thought for the day." It is ceremonial deed in the best Christian sense. Hearing the Word in the various forms it takes in Scripture—narrative, history, poetic praise, theological argument—rehearses God's self-giving to man and reiterates the fact that we inherit a history that we make our own. We are part of a community of memory in which, partly by means of memory, God reveals himself anew for the present.

Again, we believe neither that God is dead nor that his self-revealing activity is confined to times past. Therefore there is interpretation and preaching in our services and the freedom for the Word in new words to speak to our own time and place.

The purpose of the sermon in Christian worship is often poorly understood. Most basically, the sermon rehearses the God-relation as does the rest of the liturgy. It is not a piece of philosophy, handed out by a teacher, nor is it a piece of advice for sane living in troubled times, nor a commentary on the news of the day. It is an act of celebration and a proclamation of good news, using the medium of the words and the person of the preacher. The elaboration of the news that man is God's and that God mercifully judges and redeems man may find implications drawn out in very concrete form indeed. This drawing out inevitably touches the philosophies by which men live; it will often mean reflection upon saner living; it will respond to the day's news. But a sermon without transcendence beyond these things, one that draws attention to itself rather than points beyond itself (even as Christ points beyond himself in the self-giving of the cross) is unworthy. It is blocked and it becomes a mere lecture or a commentary on the state of mind of the preacher.

The sermon, since expression of the God-relation is its function, commonly begins from that other Word, the Scripture. This beginning is itself a rehearsal of the God-relation in which and for which the sermon stands. If preaching begins with some human dilemma as illustration, it should move early into the light shed on the question by the self-revealing activity of God himself. Otherwise, human questions dictate answers that are merely human wisdom and the element of transcendence is lacking.

"I decided to know nothing among you except Jesus Christ and him crucified," said Paul. "The wisdom of this world is foolishness." In such statements Paul sets down the scandal of the cross—that it contradicts our human ideas of the kind of God we expect and the kind of Savior we want. It represents the conflict between the wisdom of men and the Word of God which must often find embodiment in the preaching-listening activity of our churches. This does not imply continual warfare between cultural norms and the sharp-edged word of God, of course. Cultural wisdom can conclude that the poor should not starve; Christian social passion, rooted in its knowledge of God's love of man, concurs. But the authority in preaching is the latter, not the former, and the movement from and with Scripture in the sermonic format embodies this fact. If the sermon does not build on these theological grounds, it is a sermon neither in form nor in function. That many nonsermons have been received and understood by their listeners as being expressive of the God-relation is simply a proof of the latent meaning in the church context in which the nonsermon is set, and that God can use even the blunders of men to serve holy ends.

The sermon proclaims good news. It is one form of celebration as is the liturgy in its entirety. Because of this, Dietrich Ritschl and others have proposed that the whole congregation join the minister in the preaching task by working with him on the Bible study that precedes preaching, and by joint preparation of the sermon through discussion.[23] Although it is not likely to be widely used, the suggestion is commendable. If it is born of a frustration, however, which knows that the whole congregation is called to proclamation and yet does not appear to participate in it, the frustration can be partially relieved by an understanding that proclamation is done through articulation in many ways beyond the preaching of a sermon. The whole of the liturgy, in which the congregation can and does take part, the social engagement and the teaching and mediating groups of the congregation, which are discussed in succeeding chapters, are all forms of proclamation. They express and rehearse the gospel. The church articulates faith in its whole life, far beyond the delivering and receiving of the sermon. From the sermon to social action and back again, the church's vocation is to give meaningful form to faith for the sake of man's health—or more profoundly—of his salvation.

When we come to the sacraments of the church, the significance of our approach to worship becomes dramatically clear. The sacraments are defined most commonly as "outward and visible signs of an inner and spiritual grace," and they are more clearly the enacting of faith than any of the other parts of the Christian cultus. The sacraments are less subject to misunderstanding as mere communication of ideas; they more clearly possess meaning and power for the whole person and his community. Just because of the profound meanings they embody, the sacraments have been distorted with a magical interpretation from time to time. Seeing worship as celebration and as the church's central articulation of the God-relation liberates us from magical views of the sacraments while elevating their significance, nonetheless, as expressions of Christian faith.

In baptism we express many things. We mark our entrance into the body of Christ and into a company so baptized from the beginning of the Christian fellowship two thousand years ago. We speak of our entrance into that New Israel and its heritage of the covenant renewed and fulfilled in Christ.

So important was this heritage of the covenant to our forebears that children were baptized along with parents even if they were too young to know a conscious entry into the community. It was through infant baptism that the magical view of baptism so easily arose, and the view persists among those who are not church members who yet ask baptism for their children. It is as if, without the prospect of serious Christian nurture in the home or participation in the church, the child could be saved from something by having this single deed performed for him.

To protect the meaningfulness of its sacraments, the church may properly reject the rite of baptism for such apparent outsiders. It need not always conclude, however, that the desires of these nonchurch members stem from superstition or from social norms alone. Human motivation is highly complex, and there is often a wistfulness in the nonchurchman's request for the religious forms that should be respected and understood by the church, whether always honored with acquiescence or not.

The problem of limiting baptism is no new question. The Puritans of early New England saw baptism as a rite of the church only for children of believers. These children were "heirs of the covenant." If when grown they did not "own" the covenant for themselves (and find themselves able to recount a conversion experience), their own children in turn could not be baptized. As the fervor of the first immigrant Saints waned, pressure arose for baptism of all third-generation children, even those of "unregenerate" parents, people who were often upstanding citizens and attended church but could not report conversion. Finally the "halfway covenant" was adopted to allow baptism to the grandchildren of full church members. It was superseded later in the new fervor of the Great Awakening, only to be overturned again in most cases by less strict practices.

This whole controversy represents one continuing dilemma in the shaping of religious institutions. Shall we for the sake of incisive Christian witness restrict the sacraments and the membership of the church? Or shall we, for the sake of emphasizing openness to the world and expressing the love of God wherever possible, leave them altogether unrestricted? How can the church maintain enough identity so that it may speak to the world from a position of some independence from the culture and yet not appear exclusivist in a way that is read by the world as intolerance? The church moves between a sect-form, in which it thinks of itself as a community called out from the world to express the holiness of God, and a church-form, in which it is widely inclusive of all kinds of people and so hopefully a sign of God's reconciling love for them.

When we baptize infants we confess with this deed that the love of God comes before the works by which man might think to earn it; it is "prevenient" grace. The child is received into the love of the church, and the congregation commits itself in this covenant with the parents to help bring up the child in the "nurture and admonition of the Lord." For this reason private baptisms are inappropriate.

Baptism's symbol of water, particularly for the adult, has

meanings not only of initiation but of new life and cleansing. It recalls the exodus, the passage from slavery through the Red Sea to freedom for the community in a new homeland. It recalls an image of dying and rising again with Christ into the new life, an especially powerful metaphor in the immersionist tradition. The new man is "dead to sin," alive to Christ, acknowledging the frailty of his old self, and his dependence upon God's grace. This is one of the comparisons of Paul:

Do you not know that all of us who have been baptized into Christ Jesus were baptized into his death? We were buried therefore with him by baptism into death, so that as Christ was raised from the dead by the glory of the Father, we too might walk in newness of life. (Rom. 6:3–4.)

The second sacrament of Protestant churches is the Lord's Supper. Again, the action of the Eucharist or Holy Communion speaks louder than the words, although some words are inseparably part of the deed. Here particularly, we are forced to move beyond literal meanings and to contemplate the reality of religious signs. Churches have divided and remain divided over issues related to the Lord's Supper, discussing the "real presence" of Christ, or the real "spiritual" presence, or his presence "in and under" the elements of the Supper. In short, there remains the problem of putting into words the experience that in communion—this reenactment of the Supper—profound nurture of Christians has gone on century after century.

One reason for the power that men experience in the Lord's Supper is that here we are recalled to the central fact of our faith beyond all our moralism and our self-concern. We are recalled to the death and resurrection of Christ. Another reason is that in it we go beyond verbal expression, that of preaching or reading; we use motion and material substance to embody what we believe of our identity as recipients of God's grace. "Baptism and the Lord's Supper are, in St. Augustine's phrase, *verba visibilia*—'visible words.' "[24]

Beyond saying that sacraments act out the gospel, much else

follows once the nature of religious language is recognized. When it is said that by God's grace Christ's presence is vouchsafed to us in the Supper, it is said that we do not adequately interpret the Lord's Supper if we make it a mere memorial and ritual in the common understanding of these words. The language of the service in most Christian traditions expresses much more than imitation of the original Supper. "Take this in remembrance that Christ died for you *and feed on him in your heart . . .*" "The Body of Christ which was broken for you *preserve your body and soul unto everlasting life.*" Here is expressed a present reality, the sustaining bread, the gift of nurture for the soul, the presence of Christ.

Seeing the sacraments as articulation of our faith and seeing religious language as different language from that of physics, we can move toward less controversy regarding the sacraments. The liberal, so afraid of superstition, may reach a new understanding of the more conservative traditions if he comes to appreciate the whole of the Eucharist as a central act or rehearsal of faith. He must recognize that the devotional use of language is something different from that of the scientist, the accountant, and the philosopher. The conservative, on the other hand, must recognize the same fact, that his words are true in powerful and symbolic ways which cannot be defended in literal discourse like that of geometry. Therefore his words can be expected to present difficulties in a secular context, and to seem outmoded to many of his fellow Christians.

The problem of language may be illustrated by the controversy stirred up a few years ago when Bishop Pike, in discussing the Apostles' Creed, said that he could sing the creed but that he could not say it with a literal meaning. Christian creeds and doctrines are like that. We may speak of the virgin birth without necessarily believing that as a virgin Mary gave birth to Jesus. Some theologians have done just this. The question has no answer in terms of scientific proof, so it may be left unanswered in literal terms. But the statement of God's initiative in Christ's birth and in his life as they are seen through the eyes of faith is affirmed in the traditional doctrine, quaint as it may seem to many modern eyes. Similarly in speaking of creation, the theologian unavoidably has in his mind some of the poetry and myth of Gen., chs. 1 and 2. At the same time he does not for a moment mean that he holds to the Genesis account of Creation for descriptive understanding of the origin of earth and the living species.

All of us can "sing" some things which we could not "say" were we to hold to literal factuality phrase by phrase. This is especially true as we grow to appreciate the great creeds of the church. They embody truth that transcends mere external description of happenings in time and space.

If celebration and articulation are valid ways to understand the Eucharist, there would seem to be little ground for petty arguments about intercommunion. The rejection of some Christians from communion or the denial of the "validity" of the sacrament in some other tradition becomes nonsense. No doubt some groups will choose one way for celebration, some another, but to make rules that exclude outsiders or that prevent adherents of one group from joining with others in their eucharistic worship would seem to misrepresent the God-relation. It smacks also of a superstitious sense of manipulation of the channels of God's grace.

It should be clear by now that the congregation in a service of worship is in essence just the opposite of what it is so often understood to be—an audience listening to a leader. It is engaged in *corporate* worship. "Liturgy" means literally a work done, an office performed—in this case by the people. Such understanding provides the direction for liturgical reform and evolution. That which embodies the most profound understanding of the God-relation, that which lifts up the holiness and majesty and compassion of Almighty God, and that which counteracts the temptation to make the sanctuary into a concert hall or the congregation into a passive audience is that which is good.

Increasingly, better-ordered services of worship are being used in free churches, and deeper understanding of their traditions is found in the liturgical ones. Some congregations are recovering parts of the great tradition by using versicles and litanies they had never known before. Unison prayers of confession and thanksgiving are also providing more congregational participation. There is more use of Scripture. Occasionally Bibles are found in hymnal racks so that more active reading and listening take place during Scripture and sermon. Better music is used and new compositions in contemporary idiom are encouraged. Following an age-old pattern, the elements of Communion are being brought forward during the service to express the offering of the common elements of life to God for his holy use. In such ways the whole congregation can more meaningfully rehearse and celebrate its Christian faith. As new churches are built, dramatic new buildings express one facet or another of the Christian themes of word and sacrament and the gathered covenant people.

All these modifications are but sounding brass if they are "enrichment" to make for better performance which people merely watch and hear. If, however, they become meaningful parts of the vehicle through which the gathered congregation genuinely articulates its loyalty, trust, and obedience, the several elements can sustain considerable diversity and experimentation. Given reinvigorated worship, the church's life will serve more truly as the renewing center of men's lives and of their culture. This will happen because a strong sign of God's way with men has been lifted up in the midst of the world's traffic.

Chapter Five

TO DO JUSTICE,
TO LOVE MERCY

"I hate, I despise your feasts.
Take away from me the noise of your solemn assemblies."

The prophets thundered judgment on Israel's religion whenever its ceremonials suffered a divorce of piety from moral
passion. Jesus stood in their tradition. "Is it lawful on the sabbath to do good?" "The sabbath was made for man, not man for
the sabbath." Such words blaze a stern warning to every Christian congregation.

If the most distinctive marks of the church have been word
and sacrament, an indispensable complement has been moral
concern. Without it, the church commits blasphemy. It mis-
represents what the Judeo-Christian tradition has known to be
most fundamental in the God-relation. "What does the Lord
require of you but to do justice, and to love mercy, and to walk
humbly with your God?" In its shortest definition of God's
nature the New Testament says "God is love," and therefore,
"he who does not love his brother . . . cannot love God."

The church reminds men of who they are—men-before-God.
Mere words and worship cannot adequately do this because
words so easily lose their bite; self-deception can too easily misread the true significance of what we do in worship, snaring us
in a web of self-righteousness. Loving God is not praising him
with words. It is living in gratitude, trust, loyalty, and obedience
to him. Whenever we use the word "God" we should imply as

much. If we do not, instead of speaking of God we are speaking of some mere idea at the arm's length of our verbal concepts. God is not an object of that sort. He is the Subject who creates and claims us.

To articulate this truth among men, the church must do far more than rehearse it in word and sacrament. The congregation must live it out with aggressive concern for the quality of human life on every side. "Let justice roll down like a mighty stream," say the prophets. "I came to seek the lost and the sick," says Jesus, "to heal, to set at liberty." Thus the church must direct its energy outward if it is truly to signify for men the nature of the God-relation. The church must be in mission.

The church that finds its life directed chiefly inward in fellowship and worship does not represent what we know of God. God is better spoken of in active personal terms than in passive ones, better with verbs than with adjectives. He "calls the worlds into being," as one modern creed puts it. As the Righteous One, he moves in history to set things right. He acts in the "Christ-event" so that we may have life and have it abundantly. Service and moral concern for the culture around us are therefore essential aspects of reflecting the God-relation. The congregation that is wrapped up in itself must be turned inside out.[25]

Contemporary men insist upon this point more than did their forebears. Some even assert that ethical concern is the only way a modern man can know God. They feel that "religious experience" and meaningful worship are no longer real possibilities because the metaphysical assumptions that seem to undergird these forms are outmoded. Many people find that the concerns for personal integrity, for economic and political justice, and for wholesome cultural life are the only avenues in which religious awareness can develop and be meaningfully expressed today. They themselves consciously exercise these concerns as Christians, and they find worship to be irrelevant. "I do not see how preaching, worship, prayer, ordination, the sacraments can be taken seriously by the radical theologian," says "death of God" theologian William Hamilton.[26]

While such a view possesses some logic, it would be fool-hardy to assume that the nature of man has suddenly changed in such a way. This line of argument, followed out in pattern-ing the life of the church, would cause a destructive revolution. It would leave wide the door to pseudo religions of nationalism and the occult, for millions of men will "worship" there if not in church. It would deprive most Christians of the center from which they derive most sustenance for the life of faith.

Nevertheless, that this is a serious proposal only demonstrates further the essential place of the moral and social action thrust in the life of today's congregation. This is doubtless the front on which the typical American congregation is weakest. It is by neglecting social engagement[27] that the present-day church most obviously distorts the gospel. It is the most common reason for the accusation that the church is irrelevant to the major pro-cesses of human life and, therefore, is expendable.

Every congregation, if it is to lead men to faith, must bind inextricably together its forms of piety and moral passion. We live in a world in which men destroy one another with crippled efforts at love, with stony disregard of their neighbors, and with anxious greed for status. In such a world, the church that fails to raise a voice in both prayer and protest has suffered a tragic diminution in its understanding of Christian faith; its knowl-edge of God is truncated.

Social reform and neighborly helpfulness do not form an ade-quate conception of the church's mission, important as they are in themselves. For one thing, the tasks of reform and service are not tasks to which God calls only the church. The call to "make human life more human"[28] comes to every institution and every individual—whether the call is heard or not. If we forget this, we wrongly divide the church from the world. When this occurs, the profiteer says "business is business" as if the call to serve the human neighbor were not an imperative in the marketplace, only in church. The scientist, likewise, feels free for uncontrolled experimentation. Both abdicate their re-sponsibility for fitting their labor into the context of human well-being. There is a legitimate autonomy of man's many institutions, but it does not imply a separation of all but the church from the moral claim to serve human good.

The great task of moving human life toward its true humanity takes place through the manifold secular activities of both churchmen and nonchurchmen. Politics, economic enterprise, and social organizations all serve human good. Unlike medieval Christians, we accept the values of a pluralistic society and of a state separate from the church. The church does not dictate rates of interest, professional ethics, taste in the arts, or the policies of the League of Women Voters. The total matrix, with a certain autonomy in each sector, should serve man's welfare. There is no single arbiter—not the church or the state or any particular ideology—that can claim responsibility for the widely diverse concerns which sustain life and enrich it.

Amid all the other institutions that touch men's lives stands the church. If the church is called to express moral concern and yet is not the lawmaking patriarch for the whole society, what is its function in social engagement? A clear answer to this question will help many a congregation redirect its life so as to serve God's purposes for the church far better than it does at present.

In the first place, the church is called to be a *sign of contradiction*. The church again and again will find itself expressing reservations about the enthusiasms of the state or of other social institutions. "In your creativity and your success," it will say to the world, "do not forget the distortions that inevitably hound your work. Beware of thinking your work is more important than it is. Look at the self-interest that draws profit or power to your sector beyond what is just. Remember the sloth that keeps you from doing all you ought. Consider the short-sightedness that limits your horizons as you contemplate the purposes of what you do."

"Church" in this context means the sum of those civil servants, businessmen, industrialists, professionals, laborers, housewives, and all the rest who gather to form Christian congregations. In their work and worship as churches they say all the above to themselves about their own "secular" pursuits just as they say it to the world through the church institution. To be a sign of contradiction is not to judge or condemn worldly activity from a place apart as if churchmen were immune to the same criticism. The same warnings are constantly addressed inward to the church as well. As a community repeatedly engaged in explicit confession and intentional listening to the Word of God, however, the church hopes to be an instrument to help other institutions also open their lives to the most worthy service in the economy of human welfare.

Early in his career Reinhold Niebuhr wrote a book called *Does Civilization Need Religion?* As Niebuhr saw it, the indispensable function of religious faith within the culture was to keep one sector of life open enough to God and free enough from self-interest to hear the word of contradiction. Religion is called to point out the illusions we suffer as we work at our own pursuits—the corrupting self-centeredness that affects every group from the family to the labor union, the business, the nation-state, and do-good voluntary organization. The church is called to hear a transcendent word from outside the conditioning of its own culture.

When Paul wrote to the church of Corinth, a group rent by problems resulting from pride, he presented the Christian gospel as a sign of contradiction in strong and familiar words. By their own experience he and other Christians found that faith was a gift running counter to man's search for status through philosophic knowledge, social prestige, and the careful observance of religious law. "Jews demand signs and Greeks seek wisdom, but we preach Christ crucified, . . . a stumbling block to the Jews, foolishness to the Greeks. . . . Not many of you were wise . . . , not many mighty," but God chose you! In relation to culture the church has a commission to be a sign of contradiction, warning the world that its values are not ultimate. "My ways are not your ways," says the prophets' God.

Secondly, the church serves a function of *reflection.* Most activity in which men engage has a fairly clear objective. At work, the laborer earns his paycheck and usually sees a broader social purpose—building houses, transporting food. The same is true in other areas. Political activity serves the party; recreation enriches life; marriage provides sexual fulfillment and companionship. However, full human life through work and politics, leisure time and marriage, is brought about only when an inner coherence unites all these activities. Some image that meaningfully integrates our diverse pursuits is necessary to prevent them from becoming tedious or even, to use an existentialist's word "nauseous."

Christian faith provides such broad interpretive images and a comprehensive vision of our common life. Individuals are not called merely to seek their own ends by breadwinning and marriage. Christians understand their labor and companionship against a larger canvas. As suborders within the human community that God creates, institutions such as the nation-state, the labor union, the corporation, and the family are destined for a function beyond that of their own aggrandizement. They function within and for the good of the whole human community.

In social engagement, the church has the task of prompting reflection about these broad long-range purposes of personal and social enterprise. The task is twofold. It is interpretive—asking questions of meaning in each human pursuit. And it is critical—asking questions of value. Consider a man who works in a steel mill. An interpretive function is served when he comes to understand his work as vocation. He knows God calls him to serve the community through his family, for whom he earns bread, through the product that he helps fabricate, and through his relations to fellow workers with whom he identifies in neighborly concern. He finds a "place" for his work in his world view; he knows its meaning whether he is executive or floor sweeper.

The function of criticism is served as this man asks questions about responsibilities and opportunities provided by his job. Depending upon his place, they may relate to work conditions, participation in his union, pricing policy, layoffs, incentives, quality of product, the exercise of power, safety on the job. Reflection may prompt one man to consider the need to hold down prices and retard inflation in spite of the particular obligation to reap dividends for stockholders. It may prompt another to help his fellow workers reduce friction with the foreman, so that the workpiece may be less oppressive. All this is part of making the steel mill a more responsible instrument for the good of men.

"Reflection groups" are needed in many vocational fields, and at many institutional locations—corporation offices, industrial plants, hospitals, universities. Such groups provide the opportunity to step aside from concern only for immediate efficiency to the institution and to consider its moral dimensions and dilemmas, asking how it most properly makes human life more human. The readiest example is found in the well-known evangelical academies of Germany. We can cite, as well, the emerging industrial missions in the United States, of which the Detroit Industrial Mission is the outstanding example. Through DIM leadership, vocational groups of churchmen and nonchurchmen meet to consider the moral responsibility and meaning of their work. In these discussions there may be engineers at one time, junior executives at another, union officers and men from the assembly line. The mission is church-supported, but these are open meetings for free discussion, in places where right and wrong decisions are rarely clear-cut. In such reflection groups, the church learns from the world even as the world learns from the church, and God is served as men take seriously their places within the human community. Another such pioneering experiment, working in this case with other urban sectors such as education, the arts, government, and commerce, is Metropolitan Associates of Philadelphia.

A community needs reflection centers too. Sometimes a step outside the parish structure to a halfway place may help. In Wilton, Connecticut, the Ecumenical Center serves this purpose, symbolized by an attractive storefront office in this small suburban shopping center. On an interdenominational basis, this Center has sponsored discussions among work groups at lunchtime—secretaries, businessmen, lawyers, realtors. Through the local paper it has prompted discussion of public issues and community problems; Saturday coffee hours follow up the arguments of Friday's paper.

In each human institution there is interpretive and critical reflection that can assist individuals in that sector to understand and mold the institution in the light of the God-relation. To paraphrase a line from Paul, no human institution—business, governmental, or cultural—can live to itself or die to itself. It exists in God's world and has a vocation of responsibility to God's will. The church seeks ways to engage individuals and institutions in reflection toward the end that such responsibility may be manifest.

Thirdly, the church functions as *innovator*. In no way is the initiative of God's reach for man more manifest than in initiative shown by the church in working for social change because of compassion and a sense of social justice. Obviously the church is not the sole innovator. The call to serve the good of the human community comes to all institutions and each has its opportunity for initiating change. God works man's good through scientific and technological advancement, increased economic efficiency, political evolution, cultural enrichment. The church often errs by claiming credit for change which is not primarily its own doing just as the culture often overlooks the contributions of the religious institution. As one example, consider the mixed parentage of American democracy, stemming from both the Enlightenment and the religious quest for free worship in the New World.

Usually the church blends its own influence with the secular. This has been the story of the civil rights movement of our own mid-century. The church's power has been a crucial but by no means an exclusive contribution to the movement. It is quite possible that during the next few years solutions to the problems of housing for the urban poor will come about in large part through initiatives from the church. Through corporate structures related to the church and other community agencies, a major shift toward understanding housing somewhat as we do utilities or public and nonprofit services will come about.

A glance at history reveals the breadth of possibilities for innovation through the church. In the New Testament church there was the unprecedented collection which Paul received from the Gentile churches for the benefit of Jewish Christians suffering famine in Judea. This was voluntary relief sent from one group to another across national and ethnic lines to help total strangers. Later, monastic orders provided teaching, healing, and welfare for the poor, an important leavening of a society not noted for its consideration of the outcast. In the modern era a catalog of reforms would include many in which church initiative has played an important part—prison reform, the ending of slavery, the expansion of higher education, more humane working conditions and shorter working hours, the concern for peace. Probably three fourths of the settlement houses and neighborhood houses in the country were begun by church groups. Certainly the church has too often stood opposed to progress—in scientific research, for example, or educational integrity; we are warned, therefore, to be alert lest the church shortsightedly cast its influence in the wrong direction as it seeks to serve humane ends with its initiative.

Innovation by the church often prompts a multiplier effect. What the church begins, the culture finally adopts as the norm and maintains by secular means. The true church will rejoice rather than express any jealousy when that happens; it will simply move on to other areas where its initiative is needed. In the midst of one city's development of inner-city community school programs, a leading churchman was reported to be objecting. After-school activity like group work and athletics was a major avenue for church service and witness, he said. Leave it to the churches. Actually, although the churches may conceivably do community work with a deeper motivation than the community school program, the latter is better funded, more inclusive in terms of enrollment, and frequently better staffed. That the society at large should begin to take on this kind of assistance for the inner-city neighborhood should only be cause for satisfaction among churchmen, even when it means the church must do new and difficult thinking about the particular direction of its social engagement.

In the fourth instance, the church serves as *a sign of compassion* as it ministers in the world. *Diakonia,* service, is one of the most traditional functions of the church, and one of the most obvious implications of New Testament ethics. The church must, as a sign of the God-relation, stand ready to receive the returning prodigal and to show its concern for those who are naked, imprisoned, or sick. The sign of compassion must become manifest not only among its own membership, where the concern for the aged, the shut-in, and the victim of misfortune is often dramatic and salutary, but also outward toward the world.

The dangers in ministries of compassion are now well known by the best-trained leadership of the church, but not so well understood by the rank and file. Paternalism, which brings the Christmas basket but fails to look at the gross injustices of great wealth in the presence of great poverty, is rightly suspect by the poor and the outcast. The impossibility of mutual understanding and respect within a paternalistic structure plagues us as much in relationships across the tracks as it does across the seas. The moral dilemma of the rich in the presence of the poor could well be listed as the major problem of our era when so much better a life for all men is technologically feasible. Revolutionary movements in former colonial nations as well as the Black Power and the ghetto community organization movements are all related to this crisis on an ever-shrinking globe. In order to counteract the dangers of paternalism in its own Christian service, the church must affirm much of what these movements represent.

The church, confronted by abject need close at hand, must respond positively and creatively if it is to give earthly shape to the truth to which it testifies, "God cares for men." In the local congregation this movement is manifest in deacons funds, Communion offerings, neighborly assistance in time of crisis, and continual concern for the underprivileged.

Our affluent society has not eliminated poverty or loneliness or illness, and the need for personal ministry in the strong voluntaristic traditions of our country is not ended with the

multiplying of governmental programs of welfare. Vast resources of talent are available in suburbia, for example, where
trained housewives by the hundreds of thousands seek ways of
wider contact and service than child rearing and the planning
of dinners for weary husbands. Their frustrated search is wholesome and should not be simply repressed with barbiturates and
tranquilizers; instead we need to build better channels for voluntary service. In one suburban church 150 individuals committed themselves to regular visits in prisons, nursing homes,
and social agencies. Young people may find a ministry in the
same way, particularly in a day when summer employment is
not readily available. In the Boston area during the summer
of 1963 there were two thousand high school students giving
their time in this kind of service—visiting with hospitalized
veterans, serving as nurses' aides, assisting in day care centers.
Many served full time. With imagination and planning, the
church can find ample opportunity and strong imperatives for
its age-old function of *diakonia* in the present and for as far
ahead as we can see.

A fifth function of social engagement by the church is that
of *listening*. The church must touch the culture in ways that
will help it to know the culture's mood, what excites it, and in
what particular way its people suffer. By listening, the church
discovers how the gospel is to be spoken and enacted so as to
be received and understood. It is a service to the congregation
to "scout" the culture, and various individuals and activities
can serve this purpose.

Listening is a way of taking a person and a culture seriously.
The church takes the world seriously as an object of God's sustaining creativity and concern. In listening, therefore, the
church embodies a definite part of the gospel. Listening balances
the function served by being a sign of contradiction. It says,
"Much in culture is good and we affirm it." One minister of
the Detroit Industrial Mission, asked if his task were that of
helping men of industry see ways their operations dehumanized
the worker, said: "No. Not first of all. First we help people see
the good in their work, the positive meaning it has for serving
human need."

Listening serves also to win rapport with nonchurchmen in the culture. A summer ministry to a scientific research community announced that through its work the church hoped to listen and learn what scientists were concerned about in their work. Within the first two weeks one of the technicians in the area came to the program center with the comment, "The church never stopped to listen to us before, but I believe it should."

In the actual work of a congregation, listening often takes place incidentally through the ministry of service. Social service takes members to places of need where they learn more intimately the situation of those whom they serve. At other times listening is structured as part of a ministry. The coffeehouses so common in urban areas and near university campuses usually see this as one of their purposes. Besides service, they have in view the double end of expressing acceptance to the youth and young adult subculture, and of learning about that subculture so that the church may more effectively relate to it. Similar goals and techniques are part of the industrial and inner-city ministries. Professional workers sent by the church into such situations must listen hard and long in order to understand the particular occasions of grandeur and misery in the slum, the business office, the production line, the world of the arts. Any local congregation can profit from conscious attention to this aspect of its work. It can use its members as scouts at their vocational and leisure activities, training them to analyze the moral dilemmas of the sectors in which they are involved and enabling them to report back to the congregation about their discoveries. It may set up new listening posts such as the coffeehouses. It may assign scouts to cover such meetings as those of the board of education and the city council. It is urgent, if these approaches are used, that internal communication of the congregation be fostered so that the scouts are heard. Only then can the congregation know itself as a people in mission to these diverse parts of the culture.

Finally, the church functions as *advocate,* throwing its social and political influence to one side or another in some particular issue. The church is an institution, and therefore it possesses a certain amount of power. It has potential influence by virtue of the loyalties of its members, its professional and lay leadership, its economic strength, and the respect it holds in the culture. Whether relatively great or small, the church must recognize that it is accountable for the power it holds.

This means that at certain times, when the moral issue of a public question is quite clear, silence on the part of the church is wholly irresponsible and morally indefensible. The power of the church, by virtue of the silence, is thrown to the side of the *status quo,* and if this is the wrong side, the church's power is invested irresponsibly. This is what is happening with the influence of many churches, particularly Southern churches but by no means with them alone, in the clear-cut case of racial segregation. When such issues arise, the church is called to make clear its position in spite of loss of membership or support. The church should be a lobbyist with the legislative branch at local and wider levels of government on such issues, making known the Christian community's consensus when there is one, and demonstrating its concern for social justice. As advocate the church accepts a place as one organization alongside others, not claiming unique wisdom or virtue, but attempting to use its power responsibly.

The participation of churches in community organization efforts such as those of Saul Alinsky's Industrial Areas Foundation has raised controversy because of the methods involved. Here the church offers financial support alongside that of other organizations for the sake of generating power among the apparently powerless. The poor are encouraged to know their just grievances and to articulate them to the powers that be. Methods include attacks on individuals who symbolize power and who could act to change an unjust *status quo.* Demonstrations are launched. Leaders "rub raw the sores of discontent" until the powerless are willing to mobilize. By acknowledging that the church has power that either stands as a tacit part of the inertia against change or moves positively by throwing in its weight with a movement toward change, churchmen can come to understand the legitimacy of using the church as a vehicle for community organization in the Alinsky style.

Actually the church has resources that make it a natural for community organization. Theologically, Christians know the necessity for economic and political powers to be counterbalanced by other power. The doctrine of sin implies that no man or institution is to be trusted with unchecked power; all are subject to subtle self-interest that is present even in the most well-meaning idealism. The middle-class churchman should be more ready than the nonchurchman to affirm the good in the posture of the lower-class citizen who stands up to oppose and lash out at him. There is active compassion built into the gospel which moves the church to work for social change on behalf of the poor. Moreover, the church is relatively independent compared to many other institutions, leaving it free to act for community organization in a way that political parties, United Fund agencies, and tax-supported programs are not.

There are many reasons that churchmen are hesitant about "political" advocacy by the church. Showing neighbor love through such advocacy is only one function of the church's social concern, but it is one that must be included in the range of ready possibilities if a congregation is to be realistic about the nature of social process and about the inevitable role the church plays in it either by apathy or by action. That the church played a crucial role in the enactment of the Civil Rights Act of 1964 and subsequent extensions of it is greatly to the church's credit and has served its overall function of expressing the will of God in the real world.

If social engagement is understood as one major way of demonstrating man's relationship to God instead of as humanitarian service alone, we are helped with three questions that often occur in the midst of social action. One is the tension between pure, disinterested social service and that social witness which really has an ulterior motive in mind—"bringing men into the church." If a particular person is served by participation in the life of worship and in other work of the church, we eagerly invite him for his own sake. We believe that many will be so served. Our intent, however, is to live out the God-relation in service to men; our service is disinterested. Our work actively seeks the good of the culture and of persons in it. We know that better housing, medical care, education, and legal aid for the poor help people whether or not they hear the explicit news of the gospel. We work for these ends without any compulsive desire to say, "See what we have done in the name of Christ." Likewise in the international sphere, church mission agencies often engage in famine relief and rehabilitation without asking any credit, unless convinced that speaking the Name can be understood and represents a disinterested sharing of insight about the gospel. In short, there is no rule of thumb to tell us where evangelical communication is appropriate as an accompaniment for social service and action. Generally speaking, we trust the actions to serve men and this is all we ask; they speak all that is to be spoken. In recognizing that the church is not called exclusively to be the agent of reform, however, but rather to rehearse Christian faith in word and deed, we have said that social engagement has a particular kind of role for the church. God wills the fullest humanity for all men, and so does the church; food, shelter, justice, the arts, education, and prayer are in one continuum in this respect.

A second question arises because many other action groups are at work in specific areas of social policy and individual need, so many, in fact, that the church may wonder why it should risk the distraction and internal controversy which social engagement may involve. In terms simply of accomplishing social change the "wisdom of serpents" will usually send church members to use their energies in the voluntary associations and pressure groups that deal with specific issues. More is accomplished by these groups more easily and the church *is* spared what may be needless controversy. Furthermore the congregation must be quick to affirm that the major work for the love of neighbor for most members takes place through the occupational and institutional roles they fulfill—breadwinners, office personnel, professionals, parents, homemakers. A man who exhausts himself keeping employment available for the hundred heads of households whom he employs, or who, as a physician, drains himself in long hours spent caring for the sick (and the mixed motivations of high personal income are beside the point at the moment) cannot be judged if he is not motivated to join the housing committee of a local human rights organization. That work may be done by one who finds less fulfillment in his occupation.

All this having been said, there is still the need for activities of social engagement explicitly carried on by the congregation so that the horizontal implications of the gospel are present in the life of the congregation, and so that the occupational and institutional roles of men are appreciated and interpreted as Godward service. Congregational activity in social engagement prevents the drift of Christian faith toward mere mysticism or the otherworldliness that loses grip on the created world and the human community in which God has placed us. It also redeems man's worldly activity from the ultimate frustrations of a merely humanistic ideology.

The other problem confronting the parish is the simple question: What shall we do? One congregation confronts so large an opportunity for service that it cannot begin to serve all the need; another may be located in a comfortable suburb where there is little apparent need in the immediate neighborhood. The first congregation is not called by itself or in concert with other congregations to begin on all fronts, let alone establish in its vicinity some kind of utopia. Neither is the other excused, however, if there is no social crisis in its own vicinity, from looking beyond the near to the distant neighbor; the "good life" for the Christian is a trust to be used in love of the neighbor he confronts, and there is no theological line that makes the near man a neighbor and the far one not. What is essential for every church is that it be involved with the world in ways significant enough that the horizontal implications of the God-relation permeate the life of the congregation, until those within it and those without cannot help understanding faith as involving deepgoing concern for the neighbor.

The social engagement of a parish thus has a symbolic function. The church in the inner city may see the need for good day care for three hundred preschool children of working mothers in its own neighborhood and have capacity to serve only twenty. It proceeds with that much rather than give up in frustration. A suburban church sees the whole city in the distance, not knowing how to relate to it. The particular handhold matters less than that the church begin to take on some relationship with this more distant neighbor rather than let the congregation and the whole suburb with its splendid isolation assume that all the neighbors who matter are well provided for.

A congregation's social engagement plays back into its life at worship in essential ways. The prayers, the preaching, and the sacraments will call to mind the world's constant struggle toward true humanity, embodied in specific concerns that the congregation knows. Confession and intercession take on greater reality. Liturgical revival indeed can only be legitimate if there is concurrently a deepening consciousness of God's redemptive love and his claim on men, and this means man's concrete response in neighbor love. Søren Kierkegaard spoke of the bejeweled dowager who was moved to tears in the theater by the plight of the poor as portrayed in a play. Upon leaving the theater, however, she passed by with contempt all the beggars on the street. Obviously she was not moved to tears over the plight of the poor. She was moved by some other mechanism, sentimentality, self-pity perhaps, but not by the plight of the real poor. Social engagement helps prevent worship from being for the congregation what the play was for the woman.

Doubtless there are times and places in the course of history when all that the visible church is free to do is verbal and sacramental articulation. But in a society where there is freedom to do more, the church with a life of worship alone is dangerously frail in its proclamation of the gospel of love.

There remains the need to illustrate more concretely the process of social engagement by the local church. One process of social engagement may involve all the functions outlined above, for they are subtly interwoven as the church moves into the world. Moreover, one step may lead quite spontaneously to another.

One small Southern church's committee on social service saw the need for a common well in an edge-of-town slum where shack residents were drawing water from open condemned wells and from drainage ditches. Having met this very basic need, partly through the use of volunteer labor of the church teen-age group and partly through the community support that came following a newspaper account of the teen-agers' work, the committee began to work within the shack neighborhood by using college students from both white and Negro colleges of the city. These students sponsored weekly recreational activity for children. A student was employed to live in the area to encourage neighborhood organization and morale. Partly because of the public awareness of the situation caused by this activity, a political result followed—the annexation to the city of this section which had been previously gerrymandered out.[29]

Nearly all the functions of social engagement were involved in this simple process. That this took place in the fifties when Negro and white college students in the South saw little of each other meant that the joint work by college students served as a sign of contradiction to the segregation of Southern culture. The church provoked considerable reflection about the city's responsibility toward the slum neighborhood involved. In its own work it demonstrated compassion and made a small innovation. Those young people involved in that neighborhood helped the congregation listen to this part of the "world" in its need, and the fact that political results finally came about can serve to illustrate the advocacy which the project itself represented.

This example also illustrates questions of structure in the congregation. Most local churches will need a major board or committee specifically charged with attention to social engagement. The group serves a representative role, making manifest the fact that the church at large has this concern, and working continually to assist the congregation in this awareness. Social service and social action can and should be steadily carried out by fellowship organizations (youth groups, couples clubs) if they exist. Such groups, however, rarely engage in controversial projects because they have as a major purpose ingroup solidarity and mutual personal encouragement. Some congregations are now organizing themselves into many *ad hoc* bodies, "task forces," as areas of concern develop—committees on a coffee-house, a commuters' education project, a community lecture series, a foreign affairs study group, a welfare ministry, tutorial services. Even a single individual in a small church can serve as a committee to coordinate and recruit voluntary services, asking the pledge of an afternoon or evening per week or per month in personal service through a community agency. Clearly, most social engagement in the wider society in the name of the whole church will involve extraparochial structures. There are brief discussions of these forms of the church's ministry elsewhere in this book.

Twin forms of enactment lead men to know that the human community lives, as the spiritual puts it, "in His hands." Each complements the other; the congregation is called to witness to its faith in both worship and social engagement. God would use the church in both ways to save men from their own desperate selves and from their inhumanity to each other. The church is not expendable.

Chapter Six

TEACHING THEM ...
ALL THINGS

Matthew closes his Gospel by reporting a final commandment of the risen Christ. "Make disciples of all nations, teaching them to observe all that I have commanded you, and baptizing them. . . ." Measured against this commission our church teaching fails miserably. Dorothy Sayers, writer of both good mystery stories and provocative theological works, said that the average Christian is about as ready to do ideological battle with a well-indoctrinated Communist as a seven-year-old with a peashooter is prepared to take on a military tank.

Most men who call themselves Christians do not meet well-indoctrinated Communists often enough to prove Miss Sayers' point, but they do encounter all manner of world views and behavior patterns that stand opposed to understanding life in the light of God. Christian intelligence must be called into play if the church is to fulfill its function of making clear to men the implications of the God-relation in which "we live and move and have our being."

A congregation must worship; it must effectively signify and foster neighbor love; and it must teach. One reason the church is not expendable is that it fosters a kind of teaching that takes place neither in the public schools nor in adult education in society at large. We must understand the unique character of church teaching if we are not simply to duplicate, possibly in an inferior way, the functions of secular agencies.

Three kinds of teaching claim the attention of the normal

active church. One involves ingrafting new members from among nonchurch adults and from among the young. A second is the continual nurture of the community of faith for the sake of increasing effectiveness and maturity. The third is the outwardly directed dialogue with the culture, a task already touched upon in part in the preceding chapter.

In considering church teaching, a person confronts the same question that arises about all religious form. If faith is a grateful response to the God-relation, and if a man cannot "on his own" justify himself by work and worship, neither can anyone claim the ability to manufacture faith in someone else by teaching him. Christian faith is not a body of content that one learns the way one learns mathematics.

It is true that faith cannot be taught with a teaching machine. However, it is our argument that purely "spiritual," disembodied faith is a myth and that faith rides on expressed forms such as worship and practical neighbor love. This is why there are churches. This means also that much which pertains to faith can be learned. For example, habitual participation in worship can be learned by "practice" just as can a habitually good game of golf; participation in worship is a *possible* vehicle of genuine Christian commitment. The church has a language that serves as the medium of its internal communication—the Scriptural ground for memory and metaphor; if well understood, this language enables a person to participate more meaningfully in the Christian community. Without communication no community can exist, for riding on the language there are common memories and hopes that undergird the purpose and work of the community.

An illustration can illumine the relation of personal faith to all the content that can be taught. In a theological seminary where ministers are trained, the central concern is naturally the development of Christian individuals who can lead congregations or serve the church in other ways. An intellectual understanding of the Biblical, historical, and ethical content of the faith can be taught, as can skills of leadership. However, the development of Christian persons, the fostering of the inner strength and creativity that make for natural leadership, evade direct communication. The teaching task involves providing a whole context in which this inner maturation can take place. The interpersonal element is important, for in personal relationship, the inner man can grow. The life of the community of faith is important, for through it faith matures. The integrity and discipline of the mind assist faith, for through them a man can enter the thought and experience of others—the Biblical writers, Christian thinkers past and present. In study a man can also probe the processes by which the individual and the society function so as to make his ministry more effective. In all this, however, whether in seminary or church school, what is done in "teaching faith" is simply an invitation. "Stand with us and look," say the teacher and the friend in the Christian community. "Do you see what we see? Does God not reveal himself to you as the One to whom you stand related and the One whom you will choose to trust and serve?"

In considering the church's teaching of children, of youth, and of others who are moving toward membership, such questions as those above lead to five statements about the nature of the process. These statements can be related also to the other responsibilities of nurture of the congregation and witness to the community at large.

1. It follows directly from what has just been said, for example, that church teaching is an *invitation* to Christian faith. We issue the invitation directly in preaching and "proclamation," of course, but we issue it with a firm foundation in the teaching of content too. We cannot say, "You must believe such and so," for stated belief in response to imperious teaching is not the same as the Godward trust that sustains men against "principalities and powers," in life and in death. Important as it is, content mastery is not the central objective of Christian teaching. The content is a means toward the primary objective of meaningful and effective faith. Teaching invites faith.

2. Secondly, church teaching takes place in *communal* activity. This element also stands in contrast to simple transmission

of the data of Scriptural content, church history, and contemporary religious thought. The purpose, for example, of teaching the young and the new member of the church is not to make them encyclopedias of religious knowledge, but to assist them in finding an identity as members of the body of Christ. This fact mitigates somewhat the strenuous criticism of the Sunday schools exemplified some years ago in a *Life* magazine article that defined the Sunday school as the "Most Wasted Hour in the Week." Without doubt church schools waste time, especially if transmission of ideas is thought to be the central objective. However, if providing for the maturation of children into the community of the church is the goal, the efficiency of the church school rates better. Some individuals raised in miserably wasteful hours end up as fairly mature Christian believers. Major criticism has to be directed toward the community into which church school pupils are being assimilated. If life in that community lacks faith or an understanding of its implications in the mission of the church, the church school is a tragic waste indeed.

3. Stating a third point, church teaching takes place in the *context* as well as in the content. This is true of most teaching, of course, but it is especially the case in the church. The classroom teacher who works with children in a brittle and unforgiving way may communicate the very opposite from what he intends in a lesson on the prodigal son and the elder brother. Another way of putting it is to say that the teacher has not actually learned the story himself or he would not be an unforgiving person. The teacher has the burden of representing in his person and his manner of teaching the firmness and fairness, the grace and acceptance, the freedom and joy that the church finds in God's merciful claim upon the church.

All this puts the teacher in an impossible position, of course. Who can claim to measure up to this responsibility? The teacher is freed, however, by the fact that the reality of God does radiate through the content he communicates. He can trust a dialogue with the learner, for this learner is an object of God's love as much as is the teacher. Scripture and the history of the "people of God" have the potential of coming alive and addressing a man personally. The teacher or the group may find that the content itself sweeps them up and takes on a life of its own— the psalms and the prophets, the life of Jesus, his parables, the story of the church. The teacher in the church can only do his best and then trustfully and joyfully pray for God's benediction on his faltering effort. Further comment on the context of Christian education appears in Chapter Seven.

4. Church teaching takes place *in relation to worship.* Worship in the church cannot be expected to come naturally and without learning. Too much meaning is distilled into it and too much is asked of the worshiper. In a sense, worship is the highest activity of man; man is the animal who can pray. Training is imperative for the best use of man's other great capabilities— his mind, his musical and artistic sense. So too for worship. Training for worship involves study of its content and repeated "practice" alongside the whole community of faith. That former day when churchmen attempted to make sure that whatever worship "experience" was provided for children was translated to a language they could understand was full of good intentions and some good reasoning, but to segregate children from the worship of their parents and the adult congregation on all occasions is to handicap seriously the process of assimilation and growth. Church teaching should include regular worship in some meaningful pattern. At least some of this should be worship with the whole congregation as well as interpretation and training in the liturgical and devotional life of the Christian community.

5. Finally, and perhaps most importantly, church teaching takes place with serious attention to its intellectual integrity. If the church is to help men know Christ who is himself the way, the *truth,* and the life, it can hardly do with a merely casual interest in the best scholarship and reflection of the church.

American churches even yet suffer from the fundamentalist controversy of a generation and a half ago, but they suffer even more from underrating the intellectual capabilities of typical lay people. In a nation soon to send the majority of its young people to school beyond the secondary level, church teaching even for adults is still often provided at a level barely up to respectable junior high school standards. The insights of Biblical criticism have been found by the church to open the way for more, not less, appreciation of the message of Scripture; they should be regular fare for adolescents and adults. Christian ethics and Christian social ethics provide challenging entrance into Christian thought for college students. They can for the layman too.

Far too many youth and capable adults are lost from the process of moving into the church because in the midst of other attractive aspects of the church they have found their integrity or intelligence insulted by teaching that either talked down to them, evaded their serious questions, or was simply boring. Appalling as it is, there are, in this country, thousands of college sophomores who still "lose their faith" for the wrong reasons. They discover that the bibliolatry that was allowed to pass for Bible teaching in the church school classes they last attended is "not true." A serious enthusiasm for learning, an open honesty, and an all-pervading respect for the integrity of the learner are essential for teaching the teen-age and the subteen youth if they are to keep growing in a way that leaves them open to the commitment of faith and churchmanship. These are years of rapid intellectual growth and a part of that growth ought to be of a sort that helps young people probe religious faith as a genuine and intellectually respectable option for their lives. Honesty does not erase all mystery. It does not evade those times when "I don't know" is the right answer. It does constitute an indispensable element in all church teaching.

As to intepretation of the structures through which the church should be teaching its children and youth, there is such a range of issues, needs, and possibilities that an entire book would be necessary to discuss them all. It is sufficient at this point to suggest that present-day Protestantism has fallen into a Sunday school rut which can be modified and supplemented to great advantage. The net result of change must be in the direction of increased understanding by both those moving into the church and those outside that there is substance to the

Christian faith. The well-taught Christian is one who knows certain implications of his faith in terms of doctrine and ethics and is able to reflect well beyond the level of the man who says, "It makes no difference to the church what you believe so long as you're sincere."

Several avenues of renewal are open. Intensive teacher training of the volunteers who man the typical church school is the easiest place to begin. However, more radical approaches may take us much farther along the road to renewed education in the church. Just as most synagogues do, the church could engage professionals for outside weekly teaching, expanding by three to ten times the amount of time invested in church teaching of the young. Some churches engage full-time teaching ministers to organize adult-level learning which is as sophisticated as most university extension courses and retraining institutes for professionals.

The Ecumenical Institute of Chicago and its affiliates across the country have pioneered in large-scale and highly intensive educational processes for laymen in short-term institutes, having involved seven thousand individuals in these programs in a recent year; local churches may use Institute teams in their own communities or send delegations to the centers.

Some serious study should be a part of all summer conferences and family camps where otherwise whole weeks can be spent in "Christian living together" with little educational content. Sunday programs in churches themselves can be lengthened. Outside activities such as music and the arts can be made avenues of teaching content by an able teacher, as well as a meaningful fellowship activity. One youth fellowship was subjected to an intensive semester of church history given on Sunday evenings in place of the fun and games that had been the typical fare. The group lapped up the learning for the simple reason that the material was taught with much enthusiasm and attention to current relevance.

Two- and even three-year confirmation classes are being introduced by some denominations, taught by ministers and other professionals and specially trained laymen. Some Protestant and

Catholic young adults are spending a year or two at seminary with the plan of a lay career as businessman or housewife, but also of an avocation as a competent teacher of church youth. Experimentation on many fronts is the order of the day in Christian education.

One group of children for whom the congregation must be concerned is that group beyond the membership of any church. Released-time teaching programs during weekday school hours may attract many of these children if classes are well taught and organized; in spite of all the difficulties involved, here is an opportunity to be seriously considered. Teaching under such an arrangement demands fully professional teachers with good curriculum; otherwise negative learning about the church takes place because of poor teaching. It would be worth a large financial investment to do more experimentation with released-time programs. Teachers are not easy to find for such programs; ordained ministers are not automatically good classroom teachers, and most public school teachers come from institutions where teaching in the religious field was woefully inadequate or absent altogether. Interchurch cooperation is, of course, essential for the program to succeed.

Probably even more to the point is the question of religious content in the subject matter of the public school itself. This includes material in history, literature, and social studies. Biblical content should be taught for its own sake; that non-churched American children grow up more familiar with Shakespeare than with the Bible is a distortion of the educational obligation to teach the formative literature of our culture to the young.

At the level of higher education there is presently a virtual explosion in growth of departments of religious studies in tax-supported education, and eventually more of this pattern must spread to public secondary schools. The public's fears in this area will subside as the ecumenical movement takes hold and sectarian suspicions diminish. In social studies courses, we allow Democrats and Republicans to teach about each other. One day we will allow Catholics and Protestants and Jews to do the same.

The limitations of educating in religion apart from congregations are defined by the principles laid out in the first part of this chapter. In the public and nonsectarian school there is legitimate teaching of facts for the sake of transmitting the culture. However, unless the school is to become in some sense a church, this teaching is not the same thing as Christian education. There is no resultant ingrafting onto the religious community.

In most congregational life no clear line divides the teaching of those who are moving toward participation and those who, having professed faith, are seeking to grow in it. Official membership is the only formal mark, and in mainline Protestantism membership does not signify unusual maturity and commitment. Nevertheless, the church must sustain this second kind of teaching—that of continued nurture of those already committed to membership. God is a living God. In relation to him we can anticipate the experience of newness again and again. Faith is lifelong adventure in a profound sense. One never arrives at the point where he stopped learning in relation to the living God. In ever-new ways, God continually confronts us with the decision to be for him and for the neighbor. *How* to be for God and for the neighbor, once we choose to be, involves learning. God acts in the world through the historical choices that men are forced to ponder in the world right now. The church thus becomes a training base for its own members, preparing them for and sustaining them in the ongoing career they have in loving and knowing God and in serving the neighbor.

Because of the nature of our congregations as voluntary organizations, they cannot usually carry on advanced education of this sort in the same manner as the evening division of the community college. Church teaching wins a man neither a better job nor the prestige of an academic degree. On the other hand, the learning in "continuing education" in the church is far from dull. It is a tragic fact that fear of controversy has prevented many churches from recognizing the excitement of serious-minded study. Harmony has been made an idol by the churches at the cost of Christian growth and witness. Major controversy is likely to attend any urgent matter, and the spinning out of the implications of faith is an urgent matter. Moreover, controversy can often help clarify important root assumptions as less polemic discussion cannot; theological discussion, therefore, can be expected to be generated by debate. Consider but some of these Christian issues: divorce and remarriage, abortion, the right to private prosperity in the presence of a neighbor's or a neighbor nation's desperate poverty; the relation of learning to true Christian virtue; capital punishment; the higher "law" of the Christian and its relation to civil disobedience; war and Jesus' teaching; the meaning of a "fair day's wages" in the light of automation; psychotherapy and religious confession; the "new morality." That there is no universal Christian consensus in most of these issues is no reason to forgo them in Christian study. Rather it is reason to take them on.

There are many ways the church may go about its task of continuing education. The principles laid down for teaching at the premembership level apply readily in this sphere. Perhaps the most obvious is the community context for teaching. Small groups, gathering with study as the major stated goal, can function admirably in churches.

Two types of adult study groups serve as examples. Bible study is naturally a perennial form of continuing education for the church. It often provides the most potent nurture for lay Christians when it is understood not as study of a dead past but of a living Word. One of the dozen successful Bible study groups in one large church meets every two weeks in homes of members for about two hours each time. Most participants are married couples. All have read a brief assignment—two chapters of a gospel or an epistle or a portion from the Old Testament. One member of the group leads off with comments of two sorts—some helpful suggestions he has found in the commentaries about the background of the passage and some more personal reactions—"What this text says to me." Then there is free discussion, and words of insight, disagreement, judgment, and confession are brought to the surface. Many personal concerns are shared. The group moves readily from the text to contemporary affairs and back again. As it develops over several months,

the group finds itself planning to close its meetings with a period of silent meditation or with formal or extemporaneous
prayer by members of the group. Coffee follows.

Note here the application of principles of teaching we elabo-
rated before. "Inquirers" find the group ready to *invite* them to
share more fully the faith they have been able to articulate with
the help of the group's study. It is a *communal* activity, each
member leading from time to time, each listening to the other,
no one claiming to have perfect answers that make community
life unnecessary. (The minister, if he is present, is not the
leader and does not do more talking than the others.) The *context* of the group teaches a quality of Christian commitment—
openness, concern, frank disagreement, as well as the words.
Worship is in the background not only because members share
in the congregation's liturgy on Sundays but also because it
often becomes a part of the group life itself. The willing use of
the best in Biblical *scholarship* symbolizes the search for *intellectual integrity.*[30]

A second adult group meets Sunday morning for an hour
before church while children are in church school. It is a group
that does not respond to an invitation to a "Bible class," but does
enjoy the stimulation of lively topical discussions. Again, brief
texts are selected by a planning committee—two pages easily
duplicated from an article in *Christianity and Crisis,* five pages
of a contemporary theologian, something on business ethics
from the *Harvard Business Review,* suggested by a member of
the class, or a chapter from a small paperback, *Ten Makers of
Protestant Thought.* While coffee and doughnuts are passed
around, a member offers ten minutes of his own reactions to the
material, and the discussion is well launched. Someone makes
sure that all who want to speak up have the opportunity.

Churches that have regularly gathered such groups have ultimately found themselves blessed with a corps of articulate laymen who make able church leaders and who understand their
work and community responsibilities in profoundly Christian
ways.

Church "task forces" with social action as their goal represent other occasions of teaching and nurture in the church. The feedback from "scouts" and resource persons in the community becomes a part of the content for the group.

Additional principles for group life will be found in the next chapter.

Finally, consider the responsibility of the church as a teacher within the wider culture. If the church's unique function in the culture is the explicit rehearsal of the God-relation, which is the context of human life, the world beyond the church must see and hear this group acting out its interpretation of that context. The frame of reference we have used above can serve to test church teaching in the wider culture as well.

1. The teaching is invitational rather than coercive. That is, the church speaks to the world in dialogue (see Chapter Five) expecting to learn from the culture, and ready to speak confessionally too: "Now that you ask, here is the way it seems to us. This we believe."

In a coffeehouse where the main purpose of investing time and money is to provide a wholesome and creative leisure-time place for young adults otherwise left with "no place to go," one element is this invitational concern. A current film is exhibited from time to time, or a play is read. In the group discussion that follows, the active Christians who are present discuss their own convictions about ethical issues and cultural values with those who do not share these Christian commitments. This is church teaching in the culture.

2. Church teaching is communal activity. This principle as related to testimony in the nonchurch culture prevents us from drawing sharp lines that break the long continuum from strong churchman to genuine atheist and cynic. Many there are who do not identify themselves with the Christian church or the synagogue, but who nonetheless see life at great human depth. They may affirm the church's witness for social justice but not its more formal doctrine and life of worship. Such persons can be very helpful in social service and action by the church; by such involvement they are related to the church community. Members of the artistic community on the periphery of the congregation are often ready to assist in liturgy; many musicians

would be pleased to assist in bringing new life to the worship of the church—instrumental performance, new hymn tunes. Others would willingly help with plays or art exhibitions to foster church-world contact and communication.

In short, the enterprise of church teaching is not a matter of firing propositional statements about God and Jesus Christ broadside at the world. It is far more a matter of one community of men in dialogue with another in organized and unorganized occasions of shared experience. In serving a teaching function in the culture, the church is in dialogue with the world because it knows the church itself is part of the frail, finite, and "fallen" human world and, as such, under judgment too. God speaks to the church through what he is doing in the world, and vice versa.

3. Another principle for church teaching states that the context teaches as much as the content. The context of a Billy Graham crusade carries a sense of urgency and often of celebration too. What is wrong in the context, however, often repels as many as the content itself—hard-sell promotion, emotionalism, evasion of broader social issues, or simplistic answers. The method and context of church testimony to the world must be as consistent as possible with the message, or the message is distorted in the process. As Marshall McLuhan says, "The medium is the message."

Church teaching in the culture must respect the culture because the message is that the earth and all men, not just the church, belong to the Lord. The church must acknowledge the moral ambiguities of life rather than gloss over them with a neat, "Jesus is the answer," as if further discussion were unnecessary after conversion. It must be as open and ecumenical as possible, lest internal divisions in the church mock its preachment about the unity of men as children of God. Institutionally, the church must act upon man's social and corporate structures as well as instruct the individual conscience, or church teaching will continue to be seen as merely an individualist message with no social insights to offer men, who live inevitably on both personal and social levels.

4. Church teaching must be related to worship—even

church teaching in the world. Even as we engage in teaching and dialogue with the world, rarely mentioning worship, we must remember that worship is in the background as the center of the Christian life. With the world we speak more often in moral and ethical terms and of personal anxiety and fulfillment. But we assume that man is the creature who will find one way or another for celebrating his chief values and his identity. The option of Christian eucharistic worship is offered both explicitly and indirectly in our communication with the world.

5. The final criterion for church teaching is that of intellectual integrity. In communication with the culture, what is most obvious as we apply this test is the need for many more laymen than are presently on the horizon who have a double competence in both Christian reflection and their secular skills. The mere theologian cannot speak the Christian word as directly to a corporate manager or physicist or physician about his professional involvement and its significance as can a member of that group. What an advantage if that layman is trained, at least on the college level, in responsible theological analysis. We can hope that lay theologians of this sort, scattered throughout our culture—journalists, lawyers, trade union officials, businessmen —are part of the future of "new forms" discussions and experimentation so that church teaching in the culture may be more effective. In an earlier chapter the necessity for actual forms of the church to engage these institutional sectors is described.

Recently a group of students at a major theological seminary proposed that the school should seek prospective students regardless of their vocational intent and should provide them with a concentrated year of theological study before they went on to other fields. Two-year postgraduate programs of this sort are available already in some centers of learning. In response to the proposal, however, some asked, "Why the seminary?" The seminary, they argued, is a place of specific professional training; for nonprofessionals intensive programs of lay education should be carried out under church auspices elsewhere. Wherever it is carried on, a vast increase in nontechnical but genuinely theological competence among laymen is in order. Not only the church but the liberal arts college must challenge the individual to a commitment and world view, a "theology" through which he will understand his world and in terms of which he will make decisions and build a life. If the church-related college wonders just what its role is today, here is one way of putting it.

One church's program can serve as an example of this section on church teaching in the world. For twenty-five years, the United Church of Raleigh, North Carolina, sponsored its Institute of Religion. This program brought prophetic voices to a region hungry for them. The Institute provided a local catalyst, through dinners and classes that preceded the major addresses, for dialogue on many levels and on many issues. Over the years the program was attended by thousands who had no formal connection with that congregation, and many who were not active in any church at all. There was no attempt at membership recruitment. The Institute was a community affair, using talent from the League of Women Voters, international departments of women's clubs, professional associations, and the like. The issues in the major addresses ranged from civil liberties to the arts. The context of the program was significant for the time— well-integrated dinners and audiences, and Negro leaders addressing predominantly white audiences in days when these were rare. Senators, pacifists, labor leaders, conservationists, socialists, philosophers, and scientists were among those who offered their hard-hitting opinions. All the work of planning such meetings over the years resulted in a highly significant gift of service and teaching for the community at large. Every church reviewing its commission to teach must be conscious of some such "external" vocation.

Chapter Seven

IN THE MIDST OF YOU

Several important aspects of parish life are not included within the activities that have been discussed thus far. The centrality of worship and social engagement, however, is paramount; other activities are ancillary to them. Education helps define and enlarge men's understanding of their identity before God and increases their effectiveness in neighbor love. Fellowship activities, the subject of this chapter, sustain the corporate life of the church and minister to the needs of individuals within the congregation.

Within most parish churches, there are various mediating groups that represent one way in which the gospel may be "em-bodied." The term "mediating groups" points to the function the small group should be serving—a vehicle not for mere chumminess but for personal growth and effective service in Christian faith.

The small-group movement, not only in churches, but in other contexts as well, is based on the very human need for primary relationships—the person-to-person rather than personage-to-personage relationships, to use the language of the Swiss psychiatrist Paul Tournier. The need is compounded of varied aspects of the human self—the way it establishes personal identity by exchange with others, its need for security in acceptance by others. Particularly in a mass society where the number of more public, formal, and secondary relationships is vastly increased, and where the nuclear family has replaced extended kinship patterns of an earlier generation, this conscious small-group emphasis is to be expected.

Group process is now being studied scientifically by the behavioral sciences. The knowledge gained is being utilized in the structure of groups in industrial and office work, in training and education, in psychotherapy, and in voluntary associations such as the Y.M.C.A. and the church. Specialized leadership training becomes increasingly available in many walks of life. The language of group dynamics is almost as diffused throughout the culture as the language of dynamic psychology itself—"authoritarian and democratic leadership," "feedback," "buzz group," "shared leadership."

The special need for primary relationships in our culture partially explains much of what takes place in the church. To some extent primary relationships are established in church committees, classes, circles, and clubs. This helps to account for the persistent importance of these groups to their members in spite of activity that is apparently meaningless to the outsider. Value exists in any activity that fosters acceptance of the individual, an affirmation of his worth, and a sharing of self with self. This is true even if that activity is sustained by a group life that stands in the way of the church's broader mission and so is in conflict with other values. When this happens, the needs met by small-group life need to be kept in mind while the existing pattern is modified to serve the larger purposes of the church.

The concept of the mediating group may be used in the church as an interpretive tool for understanding what takes place in the church school, in fellowship activities, and also in administrative boards and committees. Once having understood the nature of the mediating group and its place in the purposes of the church, we may evaluate this sector of church life and see how to use it in church renewal. Mediating groups are under considerable criticism, but their potential in the mission of the church is often misunderstood and unexploited.

We have already seen that one way in which an individual rehearses his identity as a child of God is in worship. The nature of that identity is further manifested as his congregation engages in social service and action. There may yet be lacking, however, a dimension that can find very meaningful expression in parish life. This is the close interpersonal relationship among people who are deeply concerned for one another.

A man's interpersonal relationships are in some ways the most important aspect of his posture in the world. (This is not a sole test of a man; some great persons have been blessed with extremely abrasive personalities.) From infancy, interpersonal relationships mold the individual in crucial ways; it is not unfair to say that patterns in childhood shape the adult "soul"— the degree of trust or distrust, hope or despair. Thus, careful attention to qualities of interpersonal relationship is imperative in a humane society, and such responsibility, we may assume, "begins at home."

Interpersonal intimacy takes place in one-to-one encounters and in small groups. This is so much the case that it is easy to overlook wider cultural factors which also affect the quality of intimacy. Parish life is therefore sometimes erroneously defined exclusively in terms of the quality of its personal and group life without regard to worship and its mission to serve the larger society. (An ingrown affluent church with virtually no outreach in benevolence and with a pattern of worship that largely celebrates the pleasures of being snugly together with people who are just like one another is referred to as a "fine and friendly church.") When this definition is allowed to rule, as most analyses of the contemporary American church have pointed out, the church is little more than a club.

Nevertheless, strengthening the bonds of primary contact in family and community relationships is a profound need in a society in which life is often heavily overbalanced toward the level of merely secondary relationships. Hence, meaningful small-group life in the church not only strengthens the church but is part of its ministry to the world. For many busy people, interaction with mere acquaintances and with people at an impersonal level—customers, clients, clerks, and fellow subway riders—almost seems to exclude primary dialogue from private life. The most consistent aspect of the numerous analyses of urbanization is the conclusion that depersonalization takes place in the process. In the mass society of the technological age, small-group life becomes an especially timely avenue for the articulation of the gospel. Anonymity, which Harvey Cox baptizes as a virtue of the secular city,[31] can be accepted only for the more public relationships. Intimacy and friendship are also profoundly important to the human self.

To the Christian, acceptance in the primary group can serve to mediate a sense of acceptance by God. Acceptance is one limited and derivative way of stating the Christian gospel.[32] Understood on the deepest level, it can suggest part of the meaning in such statements as these: "While we were yet sinners Christ died for us"; "There is . . . now no condemnation for those who are in Christ Jesus."

If the church is called to embody the God-relation, there must be manifest in the life of a parish the dimensions of love: *acceptance* of the other, rather than judgmental reserve; *affirmation* of the worth of the other and concern for his growth; *sharing* between persons, which will include a willingness to listen and to confess weakness; and finally, a *self-giving concern* that can receive hurt by others. Without such qualities in parish life, the most specifically "religious" activity, that of worship, can become sounding brass for both the internal participant and for the outsider who visits a church. In its internal life, the church must give concrete expression to the love of God (being called as the "firstfruits" of the coming Kingdom) or it will have failed to convey the very message it exists to communicate. No parish fully embodies God's love, of course; and the gospel has reached men in spite of unloving churches. Nevertheless, no such word as "God is love" can be understood apart from some experience of human love. The familiar expression from the Johannine epistle has it, "We love, because he first loved us" (I John 4:19). There is truth here that can be translated to the human plane of personal relationship. No one is likely to reach out to others in love if he, himself, has not experienced acceptance and love. Otherwise his anxiety for personal security blocks his acceptance of others. Where possible the church must contribute to the loving nurture of persons if it is to fulfill its function of articulating the gospel. One means for this is the mediating group.

Without calling it mediation, we have already stated the need for Christian education to be concerned with the quality of group life in the parish. The principles of the mediating group apply all the way from preschool nursery classes through adult education. The teaching of the Christian faith becomes an impossibility unless understood in these dynamic terms. There could be teaching of facts in a very uninviting atmosphere under an authoritarian teacher—history, liturgical forms, the norms of Christian morality—but trust in God and such loyalty to him as generates love toward the neighbor would be quite another matter. The Christian faith is communicated, caught, in the context of the mediating group. The process is different than, more than, the communication of mere facts. As Roger Shinn puts it, with the wrong kind of Christian education, "pupils may acquire information that has some value for them, but more often than not they become better prepared to win Bible quizzes than to make Christian decisions."[33] The motivation and the content of Christian decision-making come from the broad knowledge of life in its God-related context which the church is called to express. Education to this end takes place in a nursery class where children have "happy times in our church," in a third-grade class where children discover their own creative talents in portraying the beauty of "God's world," in a sixth-grade class where children act out with free conversation the dialogue of Jesus with the rich young ruler and so feel the challenge that Jesus offers men, in a tenth-grade group where religious doubts can be freely raised and discussed, in an adult seminar thinking through the implications for modern life of freedom in Christ amid an exploitative culture in which the individual may be subtly imprisoned.

In the church, the atmosphere of learning is as important as the level of intellectual content. Much as this is also true at lower levels of secular education, at advanced levels it is not. There, academic standards are the chief criteria for evaluation, even when it means the "rejection" of some students by the award of failing grades. The parish church uses other criteria. It is fair to judge one parish study group as superior to another in fulfilling its most basic function because in the one an irregular participant raising an irrelevant question is dealt with patiently and in the other he is cut short. The Christian educator must understand what is happening to whole persons, and recognize that the intellectual process cannot be split off into its own sphere in the church. This is as true with three-year-olds as with grandparents.

One church leader, highly cognizant of this fact, reports that he serves coffee at eight as a prelude to an evening meeting of a series preparing adults for membership. He mixes with the group in conversation that expresses concern and interest in these newcomers. There is no rushing into the content of the meeting; in fact it is often left until a member of the group asks —as late as eight thirty, "Hadn't we better be getting started?" "The work of the group is accomplished," says the pastor in this church, "between eight and eight thirty as much as between eight thirty and ten."

Small groups in the church have been described adequately in a number of books by men who have discovered the meaningful dimension they offer to the churches. Notable are the recent *New Life in the Church* and *Reshaping the Christian Life,* by Robert Raines, and *Spiritual Renewal Through Personal Groups,* edited by John Casteel. Hence there is no need to go into detail regarding these viable patterns for adult group participation in the body of Christ. Small groups may center on Bible study, contemporary literature, social issues, or personal problems. Growing from the study and group life, intercessory prayer may become part of the pattern.

It is important that the group see itself in the context of the whole church. If it becomes separated from the life of worship and social engagement, the warning signals must go up immediately. When a group is maintained in spite of that separation, it is to be seen as more of a "halfway house" for people who have yet to find their way into the church. It serves, perhaps, as an inquirers' group (even while including nominal church members), an important arm of church outreach, to be sure, but lacking the traditional and still valid signs or tests of the church —word and sacrament. Certainly there is as much justification for this type of group as for a halfway house where school dropouts and potential delinquents may find a hangout, but the "halfway standing" is important lest the group enjoy its private piety or its intellectual stimulation and think of itself as truly being the church while cut off from the major celebration by the people of God and that people's servanthood in the world. This argument is important for discussion of new forms of the church.[34] It is in the whole church that the faith of the New Israel is expressed—its memory and hope, its discussion and enactment of the community's ethical commitments. An isolated, small, intimate group may minister to many personal needs; it is not the church, fully understood.

Consider now as mediating groups the multifarious fellowship groups and functional committees[35] of the church. There is a great deal of current criticism of women's groups, and couples clubs; yet most churches have them. What is needed is a clearer understanding of their potential and a realistic assessment of the actual service they now render. Much the same can be said of the committees.

Among auxiliary fellowship activities in the churches are to be found everything from the ladies' day musical program in a church of the urban Negro ghetto to the men's club of a suburban parish watching moving pictures of the latest football season of a nearby college. The new pastor approaching these church-sponsored affairs is appalled to discover people thinking of them as a part of their own participation in significant church activity and hence, he assumes, in the body of Christ and its work of ministry. There is apparently no proclamation in these gatherings: neither worship, nor social service, nor teaching.

The dilemma of auxiliary groups is not solved by an abrupt judgment on their activities, as lay leaders and ministers have often learned in painful ways. A recognition of the dynamics involved in them paves the way for more creative group life in the congregation. Parish life is strengthened by the occasions on which persons come to know one another. Leisure-time activities—in the church building or outside it, whether initiated by the congregation or not—become just such occasions when persons of the church are together. Moreover, in terms of mediation, there is some possibility, limited as it is, that in these social contacts those outside the life of the parish may come the first step toward ingrafting into the fellowship of the congregation; further steps will involve a genuine understanding of what the church is all about. For these two reasons, the bazaars and men's clubs, whether in an urban Irish-Catholic parish or a Presbyterian church at a rural crossroad, need to be judged initially with sympathy. Then, let change be initiated. Subtle distortion of their legitimate purposes is a very serious problem in fellowship groups in the church. For one thing there can be an in-group clubbiness which, toward the outsider, is the very opposite of openness and love. Worse yet is the fact that these activities may be thought of as "church work" and may consume in busy lives the time otherwise available for works of social engagement. Even when something like prayer or social service is a part of the fellowship activity, there is an ever-present danger that it may be an empty gesture—witness the difference between the typical devotional service at a women's luncheon and the Lord's Supper celebrated by the whole congregation. There is the additional hazard that some achievement of an auxiliary group—funds raised, people "won" to the group, or crowds drawn to a performance—will be seen as an achievement in the Kingdom. This is the same sinful betrayal of the gospel that is in all assumptions of self-justification.

Not only internally, but externally too, fellowship groups distort the purpose of the church. When church-related affairs appear on the social pages with reports about the color scheme for decoration rather than about any substantial activity of social engagement or education, the public is given a false impression of what the church, essentially, is up to. When fellowship activities of any sort become the activity for which a church is known in a community, there is tragic external distortion. Hence activities legitimate enough by nature may be illegitimate by their very size; the tail begins to wag the dog. When this happens, as with a great deal of college athletics, it is time for a concerted effort at de-emphasis.

There are no ready answers for these problems apart from the context of each church, case by case. Certainly money can be raised in all middle-class churches by direct giving, and this is a far more meaningful expression of Christian stewardship than are fairs. The very human needs of fellowship and of a sense of usefulness, which have been met by church bazaars, may and should be met in other ways—study groups, service projects, quiet days and retreats, the ministry of the "diaconate" in areas of community life.

Turning to the external use of fellowship activities, let the halfway house aspect of them be frankly and consciously cultivated. In other words, the church may legitimately sponsor its nonreligious enterprises for the purpose of making initial contact with those whom it hopes to find finally choosing to participate in the central life of the church. This is one purpose of coffeehouses and teen canteens, of church suppers for the neighborhood, and of children's group work under church sponsorship. The process of involvement must be thoughtfully conceived, however. If Jack Wilson comes to a men's banquet to see a football game and church membership is suggested to him in this context with no requirements of membership training, he may well be excused if he comes to understand the church as something of a social club rather than as the body of Christ. Leadership training in a church must work on just this kind of question over and over again, if the auxiliary activities are to be kept from distorting the meaning of the church as understood by its own members and by the community at large.

The difficulties presented by fellowship groups of the church are serious enough that the suggestion is often made that all parish life should be structured differently. A parish might be organized through Bible study groups or action groups with assignments in social engagement. Wherever there is leadership that can win response to these proposals, there is bound to be a renewed vitality in a congregation. For the great number of churches, however, more progress can be made through a conscious evaluation of present patterns and an evolutionary type of reform. Whatever the new structures, the dynamics of group life will play a role in sustaining church activity; this fact must be acknowledged. Furthermore, we can remember the actual service rendered to persons—whether upper class or lower, gregarious or lonely—by the auxiliary groups. In the case of teen canteens or golden-age checker clubs, Scout troops, and mothers clubs this ministry may be clear; the more ordinary couples clubs and women's meetings can serve a similar function.

It is appropriate to add some word about the functioning committees that are so large a part of the members' work in most smaller parishes. In many typical churches these committees appear to be almost the only activity outside that of corporate worship.

It should be clear that the role of every board and committee must be seen as a part of the whole church and derives its meaning from this involvement. What is to be emphasized by calling the committee a mediating group is that each committee has an internal life as well as an organizational task to perform. The norms that ought to characterize the mediating group in the church hold for the committees just as for fellowship organizations.

There is a real possibility of tension as these norms are applied. A committee may have in it someone whose personal needs are such that he prevents a committee from accomplishing its work in a given evening; usually, the task at hand and the maintenance of the group as a viable organism must take precedence over the individual's needs. However, a parish leader must understand his responsibility both to the individual and to the whole group and its appointed task. Outright silencing of such a member, while permissible in a political gathering or a corporate stockholders' meeting, may not be proper in a small church group.

It is one of the dangers of the church that patterns from other involvements—the family, the club, the business corporation, the governmental agency—are translated through the habits and assumptions of church members into the shape of the church itself. Such habits can obscure the unique aspects of the

Christian community. The sect group, which is more self-consciously set over and against the world's patterns of life, has an advantage in this respect. Although unrealistic for larger groups, the Quaker insistence upon unanimity lifted up certain standards for the Christian group; it set standard procedures in this body on a different plane from that of secular associations, reminding participants of responsibilities here that could not be enforced in a mixed environment outside the church.

All parish committees must be seen as mediating groups charged with the responsibilities of reflecting faith by their behavior as well as with efficiency and effectiveness in the business assigned to them. This consideration is also pragmatically wise, generally speaking. Group dynamics studies summarize the conditions of effective group life in both voluntary situations and those where economic sanctions can be applied. These studies indicate that the functioning of a group must be concerned with meeting the three kinds of needs to which we have already referred: those of the task at hand, those of maintenance of group morale, and those of individuals involved. A voluntary group can fail if any one of these is neglected. A committee must get about its business (task), must keep communication open and persons willingly participating (maintenance), and must be aware of individuals to the extent that no one is wrongly overruled or unjustly offended.

Situations of conflict arise in which the importance of the task does overrule the maintenance of the group. Taking the congregation at large as an example, there may be times of controversy when a vote must be taken. A time may come to vote open membership, for example, in a Southern, white, and therefore segregated parish, even if a large section of the congregation withdraws. The cost must be weighed against the need—there are conflicting values.

Leadership that can accomplish the task while maintaining the group as a whole is better off than that which cannot. In a committee an individual who is defeated by a majority will possibly be hurt. Leadership that can reach consensus without "dividing the house" with a pro and con vote will help avoid this.

If unavoidable, responsible leadership in dividing the house will see to it that the relationships with the person involved are re-established. Such concerns are good advice for any group; in the church they are a moral responsibility.

That the quality of group life in committees is a meaningful part of church work is often overlooked by those who are impatient with the human frailty which prevents most churches from becoming dynamic centers of liturgical renewal and social reform. Not only are people spending time together in the name of the body of Christ, but they are engaged in a process through which Christian nurture can take place. A study or training program may be introduced into nearly every church committee. A good Christian education committee must continually reflect upon the purposes of its work and the tools available. So, too, a board of deacons, elders, vestrymen, trustees, or stewards may spend a portion of each meeting working on issues of community importance, in direct Bible study, or in study of current materials on religious thought and practice. Such activity will have the value of leadership training, of course, but also the symbolic function of reminding the group of the real nature of its particular tasks.

Subgroups of the congregation or of the wider church are important because they provide opportunities of expression and involvement beyond that of the service of corporate worship. Therefore, lively personal involvement in at least one small group that has some kind of religious identity is a norm we can suggest for every professing churchman. The possibilities for such participation are manifold—task forces for social engagement, reflection groups at the work place, church school classes and teachers groups, study seminars, fellowship activities, church committees. Ideally all these groups have a place as spokes between the hub of the liturgical gathering of Christians and their dispersion as individual Christians to their private and public worlds. Involvement in such mediating groups can enable churchmen to participate in both church and world with greater joy and faithfulness.

Chapter Eight

DERIVATIVE CONSIDERATIONS

Deriving from the frame of reference used in the previous chapters for interpreting the shape of parish life, there are three further issues that need brief treatment at this point. They have to do with relating the congregation to the wider body of Christendom, with church leadership, and with the question of membership in the congregation.

No local congregation today can show the world the good news of God's love or even celebrate it for itself without a strong tie to the whole church. Ecclesiastical isolationism does not express the "wideness in God's mercy"; connectionalism is an essential element in the life of the local church. Moreover, because of certain inherent limitations of the local parish, it is necessary that the congregational structure be supplemented by new forms of the church, a fact that is presently under considerable discussion by churchmen in all parts of the world.

For many denominations connectionalism is understood. Methodist churches, for example, often list their officers by beginning with the bishop of the conference and the superintendent of the district in which each is located, only then naming the pastor of the local congregation and other officers. In the Episcopal Church confirmation is a rite performed only by the bishop, clearly marking this event as reception into the wider church. Presbyterian elders are ordained by the laying on of hands, an act recollecting the apostolic succession of the church and conferring on them in that denomination a status that goes with them as they move from one congregation to another.

Within that wing of American Protestantism with strong congregational emphasis, the word "church" is understood primarily in reference to the local congregation. This presents difficulties for a time when a sense of the wholeness of the church needs embodiment in the shape of the congregation and when mutual responsibility of one sector of the church for another is to be expected. There are historical and theological reasons for the feeling among Baptists, Disciples of Christ, and many of the sect groups that share congregational polity, that the local church is a complete church with Christ as its head, no hierarchy beyond that being necessary. Denominational structures have been seen by Congregationalists and these groups simply as offices for coordinating the work of the local churches. The symbolic function of connectional structure is altogether overlooked in such a view.

For such free churches especially, but for all congregations in our voluntaristic society, it is important to rediscover that the whole church is a living reality. The word "church" in the New Testament refers both to a local group of Christians and to the whole church, the universal body of believers, referred to in the creed as the "holy catholic church." Our contemporary use of the word for a denomination is an innovation of church history. We speak now of the Methodist, the Episcopal, or the Presbyterian Church; in interdenominational bodies we think of denominations as constituting, for example, the World Council of *Churches.*

Denominations and church councils are bureaucracies that accomplish things local churches individually could not do— establish colleges, set up missions to migrants, start churches in new communities, send medical doctors to underdeveloped nations. However, they serve another purpose. Tied into a denomination and its missions, the local church rehearses through its cooperation with the bureaucracy its involvement with the whole people of God and with the needs of the world beyond its own community.

The local congregation can expedite a consciousness of this wholeness of the church in many ways. It will publicize reports on activities of the denomination and of churches in general. It may list and financially support particular mission projects— a doctor in Africa, a seminary professor in India, a social worker in the inner city. It will consider important the selection and the continuity of representation at denominational meetings.

With a marked increase in the interdependence of society, churches themselves must move toward broader organizational forms, particularly those inheriting a tradition of independence. Otherwise, the meaning these churches have for men will remain limited to a very private realm quite unrelated to the bureaucratic activity that shapes so much of our common life. At one time, most aspects of life could be significantly touched by a local religious institution; now, on the urban scene, churches that exalt localism at the expense of ecumenical mission can hardly claim to be fulfilling the purposes of the church. In its social engagement, a local church is limited in what it can accomplish. How can the neighborhood church effectively address itself to citywide problems of the metropolis, or to governmental or economic issues of national scope? A strong council of churches can do this for the city; a national denomination or conciliar body may relate meaningfully to structures in Washington, D.C., or on Park Avenue, New York City.

Even at the neighborhood level, church cooperation is essential for effective social witness. A dozen churches divided by denomination and social class can hardly launch a meaningful program of social renewal or reflection for their sector of a city if they work only singly. Cooperation is essential, and these strong horizontal ties are the most significant kind of connectionalism of the local church if they can be established, even if such an investment of concern means reduction of denominational loyalties—or *because* it does! Such area "parishes" are developing in some city neighborhoods already, and Stephen Rose proposes further and radical steps in this direction in *The Grass Roots Church*.[36]

What is needed is a shift in our understanding of the word "church" so that it is no longer so parochial in its connotations. The use of the word for a denomination is helpful in modifying the radical voluntaristic mentality so common in our midst. The

Congregational Christian *Churches* became a part of the United *Church* of Christ in the union of 1957. Activities carried out in the name of the whole church encourage this consciousness. The Episcopal Church takes on a shape and a meaning not only through all its local congregations but also as the denomination sponsors a day camp for inner-city children or issues a statement from a bishop on racial integration in the schools. By employing a counselor for drug addicts in a ghetto storefront, a denomination can express for the world the reaches of Christian concern, and local churches can catch a wider vision of their mission as a result. A host of other activities generally impossible for a single church are possible to ecumenical institutions. A vocational conference can be sponsored by all the churches of a small city—involving doctors or lawyers or union officers—when no single church could manage. As our understanding of "church" is thus broadened, the support for denominational and ecumenical activity will increase beyond present levels.

Through connectionalism, local church members come to understand the breadth and inclusiveness of the people of God. Worship takes place in gathered congregations, usually residentially based. Because of the homogeneity of many neighborhoods, these congregations generally tend to be one class and one race in their makeup, a handicap for the experience of celebration and for outward witness if worship is to express the inclusiveness of the body of Christ. Even greater segregation results from the American pattern of voluntary churchmanship; people of similar class and taste and race collect in a congregation after "shopping around" for a church that appeals to them. The process usually narrows the membership of congregations beyond what it would be if church membership were defined by geographical parish areas. The Roman Catholic pattern has advantages on this count, for, except in ethnic and personal parishes, Roman Catholic churches are geographically defined.

The consumer-oriented conception of church selection so common among Protestants will be overcome only as church membership connotes mission more than self-service. We should be selecting church activity on grounds of strategic service rather than class homogeneity and the like. We may involve ourselves in a local congregation outside our neighborhood or beyond our own class and racial group.

Churches that are not neighborhood based have unique opportunities. Many city churches draw membership from widely separated areas, often of diverse social and ethnic groups. They have greater opportunity to relate to the institutions of the whole city than do neighborhood churches. They can fail, of course, if they ignore the urban problems in the immediate neighborhoods of their church buildings. They can also fail if they become enclaves of retreat from the problems of urban society. Some city churches enlist suburban members who want to support church mission to the city beyond the suburban neighborhood. There are members of city churches who regularly travel ten and fifteen miles to engage in weekday programs with inner-city residents and to participate in action programs on urban renewal. Some white churchmen are becoming members of Negro churches, and vice versa, for the specific purpose of expressing the wholeness of the church. There is no rule of thumb dictating that it is the best system in our society for each churchman to find his primary congregational life in the church nearest his home, although that is better than "shopping around" with the consumer view. Broadening the meaning of "church" through emphasis on mission will spread suburban participation in programs of city missionary societies, more support for inner-city church movements, more interchurch exchanges. Any local church seeing some of its leaders move into these wider circles must be prepared to endorse and encourage their work even though it means time taken away from the local parish.

We come now to discussion of new forms the wider church must add to its present ones so that it may more fully express the religious dimension of human life. Citing several contemporary definitions of the need, we have already spoken of the limitations of the neighborhood church by virtue of its location.

In a complex culture which is so diffuse in its activities of work and leisure, schooling, and economic enterprises, the neighborhood church tends to relate more to the life of women and children than to the life of men, more to leisure than to work, more to the private sector than the public, more to the psychological than the ideological.

In areas of personal ministry the church has already seen the need for specialized ministry if it is to serve people where they are and manifest the breadth of Christian concern beyond normal neighborhood life. With considerable efficiency pastoral leadership is provided on college and university compuses; chaplains are maintained in many hospital and prison situations and in the military services by virtue of governmental support. These are well-established "para-parochial" expressions of the church. Today there is need for yet other special outreach by the church, particularly toward the work-life sectors of society.

In Germany, for many cultural and historical reasons, the active Protestants in the worshiping community at Sunday services runs only 12 to 15 percent of the population, according to Franklin Littell.[37] The significance of the church in Germany, however, is more important than these figures indicate, thanks in part to other forms of the church. One important expression of the church has been the annual mass rally called the *Kirchentag,* and the regional rallies like it. Another is found in the numerous evangelical lay academies where churchmen and others gather for vocational conferences to discuss their own moral responsibilities in such fields as medicine, industry, politics, and education. The influence of the academies led Littell to write that the "most significant laymen's movements in the world today are to be found in Europe and not in America,"[38] and to imply that the overall influence of the church in terms of national policy is larger in Germany than in the United States, church attendance notwithstanding. One could question this conclusion without disproving the clear illustration that the numerical strength of worshiping congregations is not the only measure of the church's significance and influence.

The church, in sponsoring such activities as the German

academies or the industrial missions in this country, takes on a new form that could be deeply influential in the culture. There are baptized men and women who think of themselves as Christians as they participate in the affairs of the world but who rarely attend public worship. Still other people are sensitive to many concerns beneath the routine of daily life and, although they have no formal ties to the church, are part of what Paul Tillich has called the "latent church." The church must not pass judgment on those who do not elect the more obvious forms of religious expression; it has its hands full in mission without that proud luxury. The church is called to witness rather than to make traditional-style church members of the entire population. New forms of the church, however, may help nonworshiping Christians and latent churchmen find greater meaningfulness in their own lives and use their influence more effectively at work and as citizens to better the lot of their fellowmen. Without extending the definition of "church" too far, these new forms could be called places where the church comes into being. Participation in a discussion about the morality of a decision at law may prove to be a powerful moment of Christian witness, as may be the creation of a sensitive work of art. Worship and social action by the regular congregation are not the exclusive forms through which self-conscious Christian identity is discovered.

Local parish leaders must continually help Christians articulate their faith in ways beyond local church participation. The life of the gathered church is in large part preparation for the life of the church dispersed, the "equipping of the saints."

Most discussion of new forms of the church has been concerned with efforts in two directions. One is simply the attempt to reach those with whom the church is out of touch. The other is the hope to signify within the public world that men and their institutions are at all times and in all places sustained by God's grace and called to responsibility to him. Because the church has tended to be identified so much with the family and private worlds, these emphases are necessary if the church is adequately to encompass the whole breadth of Christian faith with its worldly interests.

These new assignments are now experimented with and urged upon the churches as other innovations have been in times past. There is little doubt that the church ought to be engaged in "research and development" along these lines. What has hurt the proposals in some quarters is the fact that proponents of new forms have seemed to suggest them as new and valid whereas present congregational patterns were represented as old and invalid. Present churches were called "heretical forms" as if new forms would not suffer many of the same human frailties. Any forms of the church will be partial, myopic, and eventually institutionalized after the original charismatic fervor, and will need the wider church to balance their inadequacies. At present new forms are better understood as arms of the church for specific functions of evangelism or social action than as the coming normative shape of the church proper. One paper for the Consultation on Church Union envisioned an ecumenical church made up both of parish churches and of new forms, each with its voice in church government and with its own ministry. The soundest definition for the church is still, however, the gathering of persons who celebrate their Christian faith by worship and by mission.

The basic unit of the church, the congregation, is not likely to be displaced. Much as we modify its architectural surroundings or its locale, much as we multiply its arms of evangelism and social outreach, the church remains the covenant people. This people may gather in skyscraper and warehouse and apartment kitchen, but it is a church when it gathers in committed covenant around word and sacrament, knowing its participation in the work of the wider church. A congregation of prep school boys hearing a visiting chaplain at a required chapel service is not a church in this sense; neither are the many hospital patients who may be counseled by a hospital chaplain, nor a group of men in industry discussing their moral responsibility at work, appropriate as it is to say that in each of these places an aspect of the church is manifested.

Two additional issues in the shaping of the parish must be dealt with, issues deriving from practical concerns at the local level as well as from centuries-long theological discussion. One

is the nature of the ordained ministry. We have defined the
shape of the local parish as the gathered group (*ekklēsia* in the
Greek, "those called out") at worship and in mission. Obviously
an ordained and special order of men to lead such a body is not
essential according to this description. The ministry is an office
established for the welfare of the church for the sake of the
church's effectiveness. However, the essence of the church lies
in its nature as the corporate body of Christ, the whole congregation to whom Christ promises his presence.

Even the order of sections in the Vatican II constitution on
the church illustrates this point and thereby represents significant modification of the traditional Roman Catholic emphasis
on the hierarchy as the chief constitutive element of the church.
First the church is defined as the *laos,* the people of God; then
the priesthood is described. Conservatives at the Council had
urged a reverse order.

An emphasis on the laity and on the gathered congregation
does not necessarily negate the importance of the historical continuity of the church, the emphasis that is the valid intention
of high church insistence upon the apostolic succession. Douglas
Horton speaks of the "apostolic succession of congregations."
The church still cherishes its past, "Scripture and tradition"
providing normative guidance for its identity and mission in the
present. God is seen to act, however, through his whole people
rather than through a self-selecting hierarchical chain of command. Where Christians gather in the name of Christ, there is
the church. The ordained ministry is functional on behalf of
this church. It is appointed by the church to assist it in its
ongoing need for order and sound teaching, for leadership in
understanding its mission.

That the professional ministry needs special training is the
most obvious reason for assigning particular men to the office
rather than rotating the leadership of churches in some more
democratic way. For the ministerial function of teaching, this
necessity is most easily understood. Martin Marty suggests that
the pastor may reply to people who ask just what it is that a
minister does by saying that he is by profession a theologian,

a theologian serving such and such a parish. The minister is called by the church to be a teacher, one who works with a congregation to enable it to grow in an understanding of life in the light of God. He does this in preaching, counseling, and administration as well as through more explicit teaching activity.

Diverse as are his activities, the minister's work is shaped by his professional specialty, the task of drawing out the implications of Christian faith for life in the world. This is an assignment for all Christian men, of course, but the process is always a dialogue of the revelation in the life of the church with that revelation Christian men attempt to know by asking as they view the contemporary world, "What is God doing?" In the dialogue there is a role both for one specially trained in the content of the historical revelation and for men whose daily tasks take them into particular situations of human life far beyond the institution where the professional minister spends his time. Karl Barth pictures the minister with two resources—the Bible and the daily newspaper. So it is in parish life; gospel and world must be in dialogue.

For this assignment the resources needed by the congregation are best found by engaging a theological resource person to assist the congregation. Theologians are not generally born; they are trained and their talents are used most efficiently by keeping them full time at their work rather than forcing them to earn their keep with a job in business or agriculture, although this is a pattern in many growing church movements in their infancy. In this there is rationale enough for a distinct order of men for the ministry just as there is for law and medicine.

There is, however, a symbolic function to the ordained ministry that makes acceptable a "higher" doctrine of ordination than these comments would imply. Apostolic succession can be a very powerful symbol to represent the authority, substance, and continuity of the body of Christ through time. That only ordained men generally officiate at them is a practice that serves to enhance the meaning of the Sacraments for members of most church traditions. This much is true from experience. That all kinds of pride and prejudice and metaphysical wordplay also come to be mixed in with debates about the "validity" of sacraments is proof not only of our human foibles, but of the great meaning with which we invest the sacraments. The act of setting apart the ministry through ordination has grown out of the discovery by religious bodies throughout their history that order, continuity, and symbolic office become part of the meaningfulness of church and sacrament; the representative role of minister helps the church express its faith.

Actually, this is still a functional approach to the ministry. The function of professional ministry is both the practical utilization of special training for leadership and the signification of the God-relation by virtue of priestly and prophetic roles given to the office of this individual by the church. There is conferred upon the ministry a certain rational authority for the sake of institutional effectiveness and a symbolic charismatic function through which the church is enabled better to celebrate the good news of God.

An illustration of the priestly, or representative, role will be helpful. An elderly woman, a spinster, who has been only a little active in the church, travels to see her sister who is on her deathbed and virtually friendless in a city where she has lived only a short while and who has not been connected with the church in any way. Upon the death of her sister the woman calls a pastor for counsel and asks him to accompany her to the graveside at an old family plot in a town fifty miles distant. The pastor does not know her and did not know the sister. Yet his ministry, as the two commit this body to the earth, is possible because he is representative of the whole church and its concern for a bereaved and lonely person; by his office he articulates for her the strength born of her own Christian faith, and she is comforted. By virtue of his role he helps express the religious meaning in this situation. As a responsibility and as a gift this function has been conferred upon him.

Such an understanding of the situation of the pastor makes clear both the limitations and the exceptional opportunities of pastoral counseling. For the pastor to attempt psychotherapy like that carried out by a psychiatrist is very close to attempting the impossible, trained as the pastor may be in psychiatric technique. Religious overtones are invariably present in the relation between pastor and parishioner, between chaplain and patient or inmate. This may be seen as a limitation in some cases, but it is the unique resource of the religious counselor. Like it or not, the ordained person, who stands beside another in the name of the church, must deal with the situation as it is. Although the minister may choose not to raise religious issues explicitly for a long, long time, his role is not to avoid them always, for he cannot. Through his listening and his conversation, he is called to help the counselee discover the rootedness of his life in the judgment and grace of God.

The increasingly popular conception of the ordained minister's role as that of "pastoral director"[39] or a minister to a community of Christians, who are all themselves "ministers" to one another and to the world, need not be rejected because of the reality of this symbolic role. Any man has ways of being priest to his neighbor. The ordained leader, however, who wishes to be *only* one "minister" among many others in the congregation and to avoid both priestly and prophetic status that sets him apart from others, is doomed to disappointment. Moreover, no matter how noble his reasons or how theoretically legitimate, he will not be serving all the functions to which the institution calls him.

The problem of church discipline is a further factor in what the church says to the world. Opposite poles of an argument in this matter are easily stated. A strict enforcement of church discipline may represent for the church's own people and for the world something of the seriousness of the Christian commitment, the ultimacy of its concerns. On the other hand, such a policy may appear to reject some persons of good faith and so present a negative image to serious-minded men who, in their own ways, contemplate the divine claim upon their lives. A broad church may reflect the acceptance of God toward men; but it may also embody only "cheap grace," speaking little of judgment and therefore reflecting little of saving efficacy to participants in its life. A theological emphasis on the judgment of God at the expense of love usually results in a sect; the sect may exclude too many who are in need of religious ministry. Too casual an emphasis on the love of God can make the church wishy-washy, signifying, finally, very little. The love of God must be understood to include judgment as a part of love. Without the combination, God's love is cheapened and weak, and God's judgment is a counsel of despair.

In order to have some shape and meaningful identity so as to articulate the Christian faith, church bodies are forced to define their boundaries. Councils of churches, denominations, and local congregations develop definitions of their own identity —through creeds, statements of faith, constitutions. The definition may be loose or rigid. It may involve verbal formulas alone, or a testing of moral behavior. There may be purely voluntary self-discipline, or judicatories and procedures for excommunication and trials of heresy.[40] In the case of delinquents the names of church members may be dropped from the church roll for the sake of discipline, or they may be retained, long after meaningful relationship to the congregation has ceased, for the sake of love. Decisions either way must be taken seriously and understood as instrumental for the effectiveness of the whole church in its mission.

If there arises in this country a strong "third force," as the more conservative and noncooperating sects and denominations have been called, one of the reasons will be that discipline has been wanting in the broad churches. Between these polarities of broad church and disciplined sect, there is at present widespread movement by the former toward more discipline. Many there are, inside and outside the church, who suggest that the churches of the middle class have become far too careless in membership policies and have rendered membership meaningless, leaving the church without a word for the world, unable to bear witness. Each actuality in the world—a poem, a work of art, a machine, an institution—may be understood to be effective because of its boundaries, because of what it leaves out as well as what it includes. Boundaries mean that many words are not chosen for the poem, colors are omitted from the painting, functions are not attempted by the machine or the institution, and so it is with the church.

In most cases boundaries need not be drawn by special concern for the behavior of individual church members or over-careful creedal tests. Rather, a vigorous program of the more active membership will move the nonparticipants to action or leave them obviously behind. To achieve discipline for the sake of the gospel in the matter of race, for example, the local congregation need not explicitly test its individual members on racial views, although the teaching of the church in membership classes and preaching must make the Christian consensus clear. The winnowing necessary to give shape to the church can take place if, in its life of worship and social engagement, the church is actively concerned to challenge the sin of segregated society and segregated hearts and is openly inclusive in its fellowship activity. Superb and dedicated skill is necessary to lead a white segregationist congregation to this kind of activity, and this may be an impossibility, justifying more radical actions by church leadership. Once the direction is set, however, the segregationist can find himself disciplined in his own consciousness without a specific act of excommunication being necessary. The church will have defined its boundaries. It will thereby have become more effective in giving shape and reality to its Christian confession.

Chapter Nine

THE RECOVERY OF RELIGION

At dinner one evening someone commented on a recent religious book. "The writer is one of those," said the churchman, "who believes that no modern theologian can honestly read the Bible or pray." Substitute for "modern theologian" the words "modern man" and you have the opinion of many people in our current age.

We are doubtless in the midst of a period of confusion as to what the church is all about. We are uneasy about the shape of religious institutions and the traditional forms of piety. We know of their frequent irrelevance and that they even, on occasion, block an advance in human welfare.

Illustrations of the confusion are easy to cite. On the political front the United States Supreme Court ruled out prayer and religious exercise from tax-supported schools and the strange bedfellows who arose to urge the restoration included Governor Wallace of Alabama, Fulton Sheen, and Billy Graham, while the opposition included representatives of most of the major denominations.

On college campuses, some worthy men are urging Christians to accept the "death of God" and are urging them to go native, leaving behind them those forms of piety which tend to set them apart from the rest of men. They have experienced religious forms as a handicap because the forms separate persons who use religious language from those who do not and hinder their conversation with the world. The phrase "religionless Christianity" gains currency among students who will not ever get around to reading the source material by Dietrich Bonhoeffer, who, incidentally, does not imply that the church must die if Christian faith is to increase.

On an intellectual plane the translation of the gospel into nonreligious terminology provides us new insight into what we want to be as Christian men. We are told the gospel means that we are to be authentic persons, truly free in ourselves and truly free for other persons—Christ was the truly free man. But then we are left wondering whether, if that is the answer, we should be bothering with churchly language and form at all.

Finally, on the level of mass culture, the sociologists look at religion for us and point out all the nontheological factors in the religious revival of the nineteen-fifties and of others in the past. In the fifties it was human gregariousness and peace-of-mind escapism that got us into church. We wonder whether, once the suburbs are more established, the country club and group therapy may not meet these needs and end the practice of religion on any widespread scale.

The man in the street may not feel these turbulent currents in any conscious plane, but he asks nonetheless: "Why go to church? I can't believe in the Catholic Mass and nothing happens in Protestant worship." As for ethics he believes he can do with the Boy Scout law, the Golden Rule, and a little of Dale Carnegie. On the other hand, of course, this man may cling to Bible-reading for his boy in school, and even give compulsively to bigger and better church buildings. But he doesn't know why and he has little evidence of the peace and goodwill he thinks to be buying at the temples of piety.

It is this kind of confusion to which this essay has been addressed. It has presented a functional view of the church. Were we to speak in theological terms another entire set of perspectives about the reality of the church would legitimately come into play. This effort has attempted to describe the ways in which the local religious institution serves needs which, beginning from the standpoint of Christian faith, we have assumed. We assume that the gospel needs articulation if men are to know the true context of their existence. Had we begun by not assuming the reality of God, a functional description of the church would take quite another form.

The function of the church is not unlike that of a catalyst in a chemical reaction. Many reactions can theoretically take place without the presence of a catalyst. In actuality, they take place extremely slowly if at all. As catalyst the church points beyond itself so that men meet God. The church's work takes diverse forms, but all of them are called to serve the end that the actuality of the God-relation may claim man's loyalty. Men may know God without the church, but it is not likely.

All this is at the same time an impossible and a limited task. It is impossible because men cannot engineer true Christian faith. It is limited because in this view the church as an institution does not aspire to hegemony over the whole of society, nor even to include all godly men within it. It does not lay claim to being the sole trustee of the religious dimensions of life, for these we know in their own ways and in their own time "will flame out, like shining from shook foil" in the intensity of human love, in political struggles for justice, in compassionate self-giving for the suffering, in aesthetic experience of beauty and wonder, and in every man's confrontation with decay and death. However, we do hold to be essential the explicit interpretation and celebration of this dimension of human existence through the religious institution. The church is a gift to this end. With so much having been done to demonstrate the ambiguities and the distortions present in the institutional church, we need now to rediscover religion.

H. Richard Niebuhr, in the very useful little book *The Purpose of the Church and Its Ministry,* states that the goal of the church is "the increase among men of the love of God and neighbor." That a different understanding of the function of the "religious enterprise" has been suggested in this book does not mean a contradiction to this obviously valid statement of the goal. It does narrow the explicit responsibilities of the institution because of the fact that the love of God and neighbor is also the purpose of Christians in many other enterprises, or ought to be, and of nonchurchmen as well. If we broaden the meaning of "church" to include the whole life of each parishioner—his social work, his teaching, his parenthood, his citizenship, his carpentry—the broader goal must certainly apply as the function of the servant church. But the task of the local church as an institution can be more specifically defined as the enactment of Christian faith. Such a definition can guide the strategy (and sanity) of the local church leader amid difficult decisions as to the allocation of resources and the general shape of plan and practice.

The church takes shape as it experiences judgment of its overpious and quiescent worship, its wasted energies, or its ingrown fellowship in such ways that it realizes they have not genuinely signified and embodied the gospel. A familiar text from an account of a healing by Jesus, "The sabbath was made for man, not man for the sabbath," frees us from the legalism of compulsive religion. We are freed from dead religious forms for work at servanthood toward the world.

In rebellion against empty form we have heard fairly well the message, "The law is dead." We have not apprehended as profoundly, however, the other half of freedom on which Paul bases the ending of the law: "You are now alive in Christ."

"The sabbath was made for man." We shall misread the text if we translate, "The sabbath is best forgotten." The church, with all its ambiguities, is an article of faith and a gift of God for man. Paul calls the law a custodian and a tutor, and we may use his words to define the essential role of the institutional church and religious form as well. So long as we leave them open to the Holy Spirit, God uses these shapes of the church to save men. To extend the words of Heschel, "on the ridges and the slopes of the liturgy," in the process of social engagement, in the teaching and mediating groups of parish life, through the whole life of the whole church, we are made by God into beings who pray and who love, and mankind is moved toward the salvation that comes in knowing God.

NOTES

1. Karl Barth, *Epistle to the Romans,* 6th ed., p. 333.

2. Because this book is written primarily for those concerned with the local church and because it considers the local congregation an essential part of the actualized Christian church understood in the doctrinal sense, the lower case "c" will be used almost exclusively, even where the dominant meaning would seem to be "Church" rather than "church."

3. Colin W. Williams, *Where in the World?* p. 83.

4. Peter Berger, *The Noise of Solemn Assemblies,* see especially pp. 90–104.

5. *Ibid.,* pp. 102–103.

6. Generally speaking, rural and central-city areas suffered a net loss while the country as a whole, thanks to the growth in smaller cities and the suburbs, experienced the largest decennial increase ever, and the largest rate since 1900–1910.

7. John R. Seeley, R. Alexander Sim, and Elizabeth W. Loosley, *Crestwood Heights.*

8. Barth, *op. cit.,* p. 333.

9. II Corinthians 4:7. The passage is used for the title of James Gustafson's book on the church as a human institution, an analysis of all the social processes that sustain the church's life and are at the same time unavoidable vehicles for the life of faith.

10. Martin E. Marty, *The New Shape of American Religion,* p. 122.

11. Paul Tillich, *Systematic Theology,* Vol. III, p. 168.

12. See, among others, Gibson Winter, *The New Creation as Metropolis.* See also, Chapter Eight of the present book.

13. Martin Thornton, *Pastoral Theology*, p. 62.

14. "Pelagianism arises," says Thornton (p. 72), "as soon as evangelism in the sense of recruitment is regarded as the main work of either priesthood or corporate parish."

15. *Ibid.*, p. 68.

16. *Ibid.*, pp. 34 and 80.

17. Abraham Joshua Heschel, *Man's Quest for God*, pp. 23, 32–33.

18. Emile Durkheim, *The Elementary Forms of Religious Life.*

19. We look "from our human side of things" in developing this philosophy of the church rather than from within the more technical theological language of the church so that the man "near the door" who is not wholly acclimated to the God-talk of the church may participate in the discussion. In the language of faith we could speak of worship as a response to God that we are enabled to make only by God's grace. We could speak, as does Paul, of the Spirit's praying through us. We might use language of this sort: "The subject who acts in the worship service is the risen Lord, and it is He who forms the believers into one body with Himself through the Holy Spirit" (Dietrich Ritschl, *A Theology of Proclamation*, p. 86). We have set ourselves to an assignment more apologetic in intent, for in many local churches the governing assumptions are better reached for dialogue by the use of secular language.

Paul Van Buren writes on "The Secular Meaning of the Gospel," translating into nontheological or "secular" language and concepts the process of the believer's experience of freedom in Christ. Our understanding at this point and later might be seen as a "secular interpretation" of worship and of parish life.

20. John Williamson Nevin, *The Mystical Presence and Other Writings on the Eucharist*, pp. 25–26.

21. Tillich, *Systematic Theology*, Vol. I, p. 267.

22. An analogy suggested by Prof. J. N. Hartt.

23. *The Christian Century*, January 19, 1965, pp. 75 ff.

See also, Horst Symanowski, *The Christian Witness in an Industrial Society*, for a German example of sermon seminars.

24. This sentence is from Raymond Abba's useful, small book *Principles of Christian Worship*, p. 139.

25. See, for example, a book by this title: *The Church Inside Out*, by Johannes Hoekendijk.

26. Thomas J. J. Altizer and William Hamilton, *Radical Theology and the Death of God*.

27. The term is from Peter Berger, *op. cit.*, and includes all forms of social service, social action, "dialogue" with the culture, and "Christian presence" in it. These four categories in the second portion of Berger's book are helpfully set forth.

28. The expression is Paul Lehmann's statement of the goal of Christian ethics, in *Ethics in a Christian Context*.

29. *Minutes*, August, 1961, Columbus, Ohio, pp. 25 ff.

30. See Robert A. Raines's *New Life in the Church* for a full and excellent discussion of meaningful Bible study groups in one strong congregation.

31. Harvey Cox, *The Secular City*, pp. 39 ff.

32. See the strong and well-known sermon, "You Are Accepted" in Paul Tillich, *The Shaking of the Foundations*, pp. 153 ff.

33. Roger L. Shinn, *The Educational Mission of Our Church*, p. 16.

34. See Chapter Eight below.

35. This chapter will use the term "committees" for the various decision-making and program-planning instruments of a parish—boards, commissions, and the like.

36. Stephen Rose, *The Grass Roots Church*, Ch. 5.

37. Franklin Littell, *The German Phoenix*.

38. *Ibid.*, p. 152.

39. Cf. H. Richard Niebuhr, with Daniel Day Williams and James M. Gustafson, *The Purpose of the Church and Its Ministry*.

40. Paul Tillich (*Systematic Theology,* Vol. III, p. 176) says that the word "heresy" is probably beyond recapture because of its connotations. What is meant by it here is opinion so far outside the general consensus of the institution as to cripple its effectiveness if not explicitly ruled "out of bounds."

BIBLIOGRAPHY

Abba, Raymond, *Principles of Christian Worship*. Oxford University Press, Inc., 1960.

Altizer, Thomas J. J., and Hamilton, William, *Radical Theology and the Death of God*. The Bobbs-Merrill Company, Inc., 1966.

Barth, Karl, *Epistle to the Romans,* tr. from the 6th ed. by E. C. Hoskyns. London: Oxford University Press, 1933.

Berger, Peter, *The Noise of Solemn Assemblies*. Doubleday & Company, Inc., 1961.

Casteel, John L. (ed.), *Spiritual Renewal Through Personal Groups*. Association Press, 1957.

Cox, Harvey, *The Secular City*. The Macmillan Company, 1966.

Durkheim, Emile, *The Elementary Forms of Religious Life,* tr. by J. W. Swain. Collier Books, The Macmillan Company, 1961.

Gustafson, James M., *Treasure in Earthen Vessels: The Church as a Human Community*. Harper & Row, Publishers, Inc., 1961.

Herberg, Will, *Protestant—Catholic—Jew: An Essay in American Religious Sociology*. Doubleday & Company, Inc., 1960.

Heschel, Abraham Joshua, *Man's Quest for God*. Charles Scribner's Sons, 1954.

Hoekendijk, Johannes, *The Church Inside Out*. The Westminster Press, 1966.

Lehmann, Paul, *Ethics in a Christian Context*. Harper & Row, Publishers, Inc., 1963.

Littell, Franklin, *The German Phoenix: Men and Movements in the Church in Germany*. Doubleday & Company, Inc., 1960.

Marty, Martin E., *The New Shape of American Religion.* Harper & Brothers, 1959.

Nevin, John Williamson, *The Mystical Presence and Other Writings on the Eucharist,* ed. by Bard Thompson and George Bricker. United Church Press, 1966.

Niebuhr, H. Richard, with Williams, Daniel Day, and Gustafson, James M., *The Purpose of the Church and Its Ministry: Reflections on the Aims of Theological Education.* Harper & Brothers, 1965.

Raines, Robert A., *New Life in the Church.* Harper & Brothers, 1961.

———— *Reshaping the Christian Life.* Harper & Row, Publishers, Inc., 1964.

Ritschl, Dietrich, *A Theology of Proclamation.* John Knox Press, 1960.

Robinson, John A. T., *Honest to God.* The Westminster Press, 1963.

Rose, Stephen, *The Grass Roots Church: A Manifesto for Protestant Renewal.* Holt, Rinehart and Winston, Inc., 1966.

Seeley, John R., Sim, R. Alexander, and Loosley, Elizabeth W., *Crestwood Heights.* Basic Books, Inc., Publishers, 1956.

Shinn, Roger L., *The Educational Mission of Our Church.* United Church Press, 1962.

Symanowski, Horst, *The Christian Witness in an Industrial Society,* tr. by George H. Kehm. The Westminster Press, 1964.

Thornton, Martin, *Pastoral Theology, A Reorientation.* London: S.P.C.K., 1956.

Tillich, Paul, *The Shaking of the Foundations.* London: SCM Press, Ltd., 1954.

———— *Systematic Theology,* Vol. I, 1951; Vol. II, 1957; Vol. III, 1963. The University of Chicago Press.

Vahanian, Gabriel, *The Death of God.* George Braziller, Inc., 1961.

Van Buren, Paul, *The Secular Meaning of the Gospel.* The Macmillan Company, 1963.

Whyte, William H., Jr., *The Organization Man.* Anchor Books, Doubleday & Company, Inc., 1957.

Williams, Colin W., *What in the World?* National Council of the Churches of Christ in the U.S.A., 1965.

———— *Where in the World?* National Council of the Churches of Christ in the U.S.A., 1963.

Winter Gibson, *The New Creation as Metropolis.* The Macmillan Company, 1963.